THE
UNKNOWN
SOUTH of
FRANCE

A History Buff's Guide

THE UNKNOWN SOUTH of FRANCE

❧

A History Buff's Guide

Henry and Margaret Reuss

HARVARD COMMON PRESS
HARVARD AND BOSTON
MASSACHUSETTS
1991

The Harvard Common Press
535 Albany Street
Boston, Massachusetts 02118

Printed in the United States of America

Library of Congress Cataloging-in-Publication Data

Reuss, Henry S.
   The unknown south of France : a history buff's guide /
by Henry S. Reuss and Margaret M. Reuss.
       p.   cm.
   Includes index.
   ISBN 1-55832-030-X : $12.95
   1. France, Southern — Description and travel — Guidebooks. 2. Historic sites — France, Southern — Guidebooks.   I. Reuss, Margaret M. II. Title.
DC607.3.R45 1991
914.4 804839 — dc20   90-47384
                                                                           CIP

To the people of the Midi
who remember their history

Contents

Preface

A S suddenly as any invader, we appeared in the south of France a few years ago. Having reached what the French call the third age, we were looking for a place full of magic and beauty, not yet swamped with other visitors.

We discovered such a place one day as we descended from a high limestone plateau—the *causse*—to the river Lot below. There, at the last bend in the road, appeared the ruin of a tower—four crumbling walls, roof and windows gone, on the ground floor a fig tree growing next to a flowing spring.

The tower was known as the Tonkin House because its last owner had gone off to the colonial wars in Indochina more than a century ago and never returned. In ruins, it had long since reverted to the commune.

The communal council presently ratified a sale, and we promptly engaged the redoubtable master mason François Bariviera (who will reappear in chapter 11, as a hero of the Resistance) to rejuvenate our tower. Meanwhile we set to work civilizing the splendid wild boxwood, hawthorn, roses, clematis, and honeysuckle that threatened to choke us. And we soon became summer members in good standing of the little hillside community.

Using the tower as our base for exploration, we quickly found that the Midi's caves and rocks, gardens and farmhouses, castles and churches all had stories to tell. The actors were cave people, Gauls and Romans, priests and pilgrims, Cathars and Camisards, troubadours and pilgrims, French routiers and English Free Companies, builders and destroyers. Between the long eras of darkness, they managed to achieve three Golden Ages—of cave art, of Roman peace, and of Christian faith with a troubadour and a heretical counterpoint.

We observed, digested, revised. When the artifacts of history are everywhere to be seen, history makes a perfect matrix for travel. To observe the first human skull and the shelter where it was found; to marvel at the cave paintings; to find in the deep woods standing stones 3,000 years old; to trace on the ground the battlefield where Caesar defeated the Gauls; to gaze in wonder at Roman temples and aqueducts and amphitheaters; to picnic on the heights overlooking the pilgrimage monastery of Conques; to shop at the street-fair surrounding the great Romanesque St. Sernin at Toulouse; to dream of troubadour songs in the music room at the château of Puivert; to inspect the mushrooms offered for sale in the arcaded square of the fortified bastide of Monpazier; to hear Renaissance music in the castle of Cénevières; to read in Montaigne's library his mottos for an inquiring mind; to walk in the home towns of Gambetta and Jaurès; to discover the hideouts of the Resistance in World War II—all this is to experience history.

The stones of southern France—limestone, volcanic lava, sandstone, granite—that have sheltered and protected its people for many millennia have proved extraordinarily durable. In greater or lesser degree, they have survived the onslaughts of the barbarians, Simon de Montfort and his heretic exterminators, Richard the Lion-Hearted and the Black Prince in their dynastic wars, Catholic and Protestant zealots in the wars of religion, Cardinal Richelieu's demolition squads, Revolutionary mobs, and nineteenth-century building contractors. Mostly, the stone structures are still around to tell their tales. Indeed, in the last twenty years, skillful restoration has made the past much more accessible.

It must be conceded that history is easier to digest when presented in a lovely setting. The Midi, with its natural beauty, its noble architecture, its hospitable people, its artistic riches, its heavenly food and drink, provides a happy framework from which to view its history.

We write about the area generally south of the Limoges-Lyon-Grenoble line, once called Aquitaine, Provence, and Languedoc. Most of it is dominated by rivers: flowing west toward the Atlantic, the Dordogne and its tributary Vézère, the Lot and its tributary Célé, the Aveyron, the Tarn, and the Garonne; flowing north, the Allier and the Loire; flowing south toward the Mediterranean, the Rhône. Most of it is relatively unknown to those southbound travelers who are drawn by the seductions of the Mediterranean shores.

Each chapter focuses on a specific period in history, then proposes a little tour of one to four days ("Visiting...") to sample that history, providing suggestions for food and lodging ("E" indicates expensive), as well as a map of the area. (Unless otherwise noted, each of the establishments named is a combined hotel and restaurant.) This book considers history the best introduction to the region for both the armchair reader and the on-the-spot visitor. Since it by no means attempts to cover "everything," some may wish to supplement it with one of the detailed guides mentioned in the Afterword, particularly the green Michelins.

The traveler will find threads of continuity running through the 400,000 years of history that the stones have preserved— the community between humanity and nature; the emergence of women as a strong and equal force; the age-old desire for local autonomy over outside centralization; the quest for beauty in ordinary life; the persistence of memory; and devotion to the Revolution's ideals of liberty, equality, and fraternity.

ONE

❦

The Pyrénées: Cradle of Prehistory

(circa 400,000 B.C.)

M A N ' S most remote roots lie in the gorges of East Africa. But the rock shelters of southern France offer us uniquely accessible evidence of humanity's long development. These rock shelters occur in the great sedimentary basin between the volcanic mountains of the Massif Central and the bedrock of the Pyrénées. As you move from the low plains of the Atlantic coast toward the Massif Central, you come to rolling plateaus of limestone, permeated by underground rivers, caves, rock shelters. These calcareous plateaus were formed aeons ago when the Atlantic covered the basin, depositing shellfish and other marine minutiae.

Long before humans inhabited this plateau, their most distant predecessors inhabited Africa. There, in the Olduvai Gorge in Tanzania, anthropologists have recently unearthed the three- or four-million-year-old bones of what may be modern man's closest ancestor—the Leakeys some jaws and teeth, Dr. Donald Johanson the entire skeleton of "Lucy," a

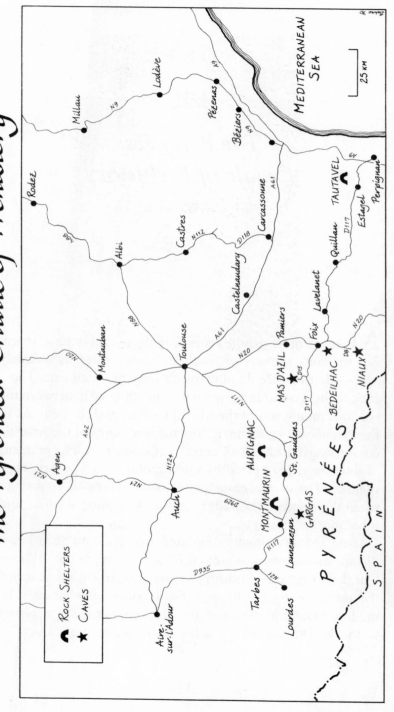

The Pyrénées: Cradle of Prehistory

Legend:
- ⌒ Rock Shelters
- ★ Caves

25 km

MEDITERRANEAN SEA

Mediterranean locations: Millau, Lodève, Pézenas, Béziers, Rodez, Albi, Castres, Castelnaudary, Carcassonne, Tautavel, Quillan, Estagel, Perpignan, Lavelanet, Foix, Pamiers, Mas d'Azil, Bedeilhac, Niaux, Toulouse, Montauban, Aurignac, St. Gaudens, Montmaurin, Gargas, Agen, Auch, Lannemezan, Tarbes, Lourdes, Aire-sur-l'Adour

PYRÉNÉES

SPAIN

Roads: N9, N88, N112, D118, A61, D117, D9, N20, N124, A62, N21, N124, D929, N117, D935, 12N

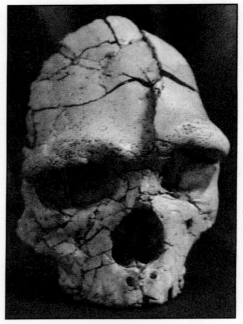

Tautavel Man
(Photo: Musée de Tautavel)

three-foot-six-inch female. Other representatives of *Homo erectus* made their way, walking upright, from Africa to Asia and Europe.

The first evidence of their presence in western Europe is indirect—accumulations of tools and animal bones on the floors of caves and rock shelters, the oldest dating back some 700,000 years. Finally *Homo erectus* appears directly on the scene in the Pyrenean foothills.

Near Tautavel, fifteen miles northwest of Perpignan, a team led by the paleontologist Henry de Lumley in 1971 uncovered a skeletal face at the Caune d'Arago, a rock shelter 250 feet above a mountain stream. Carbon dating places it at 455,000 years old. Other bits later discovered nearby have enabled the reconstruction of a skull.

Tautavel Man has a receding forehead and thick folds over his eye sockets. "He could stand erect," observed an anthropologist, "with perhaps a slight tendency to lean forward!" Tautavel Man could not make fire and may have stooped to cannibalism on occasion.

More than a hundred volunteers are assisting in the continuing excavations, and the team gladly accepts volunteers. You can see the reconstructed skull at the Tautavel Museum. Next door is a wine cooperative, where we bought the excellent Tautavel reds and white and the delicious Rivesaltes dessert wine.

A second site is the grotto of Montmaurin at the southern end of Gascony in the "Little Pyrénées" southwest of Toulouse, a land of rippling streams and forested foothills. Here, in 1941, two avid archaeologists, the count and countess of St. Périer, unearthed a 350,000-year-old human jaw. The tiny museum at Montmaurin was closed on the Sunday we visited the site, but pretty nine-year-old Rafaelle from the farmhouse across the way smilingly agreed to get the key from her mother, the custodian. Rafaelle, pointing out the ancient mandible in the showcase, commented, "Except for his undershot jaw, not a bad-looking fellow!"

Homo erectus seems to have had two lines of descendants—Neanderthal man (named for the valley in Germany where his remains were first dug up), who lived from 100,000 to 30,000 B.C., and *Homo sapiens*, Cro-Magnon, the first modern man.

Neanderthal was heavy-browed, short, and powerful, with a brain about the size of modern man's. He made fire, buried his dead, and made tools and utensils more sophisticated than those of his predecessors. But he left no trace of having

Rafaelle at Montmaurin

possessed the gifts of *Homo sapiens*—the ability to reason, to create art, to make measurements.

The Neanderthal race managed to survive and spread despite the wild climatic swings ensuing from the glaciers advancing and receding over Europe. Some hundred Neanderthal fossils have been discovered in France, ranging from full skeletons preserved in caves to single teeth. A 50,000-year-old grave containing the skeleton of a three-year-old child, found in the cave of Roc de Marsal in the Dordogne, has been removed to the National Museum of Prehistory at Les Eyzies. The cave itself, like other Neanderthal sites that have been picked over by archaeologists, is no longer worth seeing.

The Neanderthals apparently died out. Perhaps *Homo sapiens*, on the move from Africa via the Middle East, took over their caves, like so many Yuppies gentrifying an area. Skeletons of *Homo sapiens*, our true ancestors, were discovered, and then sadly lost, at Aurignac, near Montmaurin. There, in 1852, a construction worker uncovered a burying ground containing a number of apparently human skeletons. Ashamed of disturbing the dead, he gave them a decent reburial in the neighboring cemetery, where they lost their identity forever.* Even though you cannot see the skeletons at Aurignac, however, the rock shelter where they were found is worth visiting. Moreover, the Prehistory Museum near the *mairie* contains crude tools and engraved objects that were found nearby and date from the late Old Stone Age, 35,000 to 10,000 B.C.

---

* Such respect for the bones of a historic ancestor, however exasperating to the archaeologist, seems to be customary. Jean Fantangié of Cahors, the venerable founder of the Quercy Speleological Association, wrote in the *Dépêche du Midi* of Toulouse of exploring a subterranean river in the valley of the Vers, a tributary of the Lot: "Our day was spoiled when we discovered a human skull and bones." News of the discovery created "a strong emotion" in the neighboring villages, and the gendarmerie made inquiries. Three years later, the excitement having died down, Fantangié concluded: "Our city having no Potter's Field, I interred the sad remains in our family tomb, where they may be found today."

In 1860, eight years after the discovery of the Aurignac bones, the Gascon paleontologist Edward Lartet (1801–1871) ransacked the rubble around the shelter. He found no skeletons but concluded that those removed were the first modern men to be unearthed. He dubbed their age the Aurignacian, and his classification of these ages of prehistory, based on the place names in southwest France—Mousterian, Aurignacian, Magdalenian—survives today.

Lartet transferred his digging to the Vézère area and was alive when his theories were vindicated by the discovery in 1869 of Cro-Magnon, the most famous prehistoric man of all. Construction workers building the Périgueux-Agen railway line uncovered three skeletons under the right of way at Les Eyzies on the Vézère, a tributary of the Dordogne. Anthropologists constructed from them what they called Cro-Magnon man. Cro-Magnon, and his first cousins, the lost skeletons of Aurignac, appeared in France some 35,000 years ago. With them, the fascinating history of man as reasoner, as artist, and as worshipper begins.

Visiting the Pyrenean Prehistoric Sites

Tautavel is on the edge of Roussillon, the province torn for centuries between autonomy, Spain, and France. It has been French since the Treaty of the Pyrénées in 1659 established the mountains as the frontier with Spain. But its country folk still speak Catalan, one of the Languedocian tongues, to each other and tune in to the Catalan-speaking Barcelona radio.

Perpignan would be a good headquarters for your stay in Pyrénées country. It is fifteen miles southeast of Tautavel, and on your way from the digs you could see the massive and completely preserved medieval fortress of Salses. For Perpignan hotels, try the inexpensive de France, the more expensive Park, or the charmingly furnished de la Loge; for restaurants, the moderate François Villon or the pricier Delcros.

Perpignan is a pretty little city. On its Place de la Loge are its Gothic/Renaissance bourse, its city hall, and its McDonald's. On several nights every week in the summer, you can see the picturesque Catalan Sardana danced there. Other sights are the Cathedral of St. Jean, the Palace of the Kings of Majorca, the citadel, and Le Castillet, the city's ancient gateway.

A short drive south brings you to Collioure, one of the few remaining unspoiled fishing ports and beaches on the French Mediterranean. The fishing industry survives, though the anchovies are running fewer today. There are a number of reasonably priced hotels on the quai, and the fine restaurant, La Balette (E), on a hill overlooking the port.

The N116 west from Perpignan gives access to the splendid monasteries of St. Michel-de-Cuxa, where concerts are held every summer in memory of Pablo Casals, who lived in nearby Prades, and St. Martin-du-Canigou. The nearby mountain spa of Molitg-les-Bains boasts the Château de Riell (E).

Another well-known spa is Amélie-les-Bains, on the D115 southwest of Perpignan, with its scores of hotels. High in the nearby mountains are the frontier forts of Prats-de-Mollo and Mont-Louis, the latter still used by the French paratroops.

For the archaeological sites and museums at Aurignac and Montmaurin, the Cerf at Aurignac and the Dupont at Castelnau-Magnoac would be good places for the night.

TWO

❧

The Dordogne-Vézère-Célé Valleys: Artists of the Cave

(35,000 to 7,000 B.C.)

WITHIN a forty-mile stretch, at Les Eyzies on the Vézère, at Cougnac near Gourdon in the valley of the Dordogne, and at Cabrerets on the Célé, the traveler may see where Cro-Magnon man, the world's first artist, appeared some 35,000 years ago.

M. Cro-Magnon had a large head, short arms, and a jaw worthy of the name. More delicate physically than Neanderthal, he had larger frontal lobes. He could think, and think artistically. This intelligent person made his home in the rock shelters, found his food and clothing, fashioned primitive tools, and deep in the grottoes created works of art that still delight the eye and thrill the senses.

Geography clearly was working for him. This is an area of mild winters, with spring and fall rain and little snow. Even during the last Ice Age, which lasted roughly from 90,000 to 7,000 B.C., plenty of grasses and other food were still available for the big herbivores—reindeer, mastodon, bison, horse,

The Dordogne-Vézère-Célé Valleys: Artists of the Cave

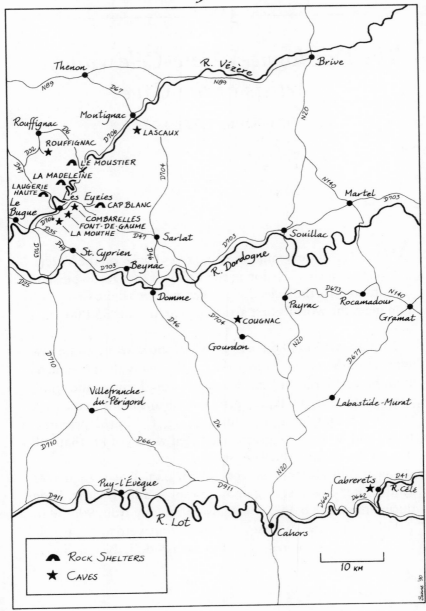

ROCK SHELTERS

★ CAVES

10 KM

cattle—driven downward by the mountain glaciers. There were caves for shelter and art and quantities of flint and bone for toolmaking. Rivers and forests yielded fish and game. This ideal environment explains the abundance of shelters, bones, tools, and paintings that have been unearthed.

Cro-Magnon's diet was eclectic. When he could kill a live horse, reindeer, or bison—or when he found a dead one—he had meat. Without cooking utensils, he scorched it over the fire or ate it raw. He could grow no crops but no doubt foraged wild nuts and fruits—walnuts, chestnuts, apples, blackberries (the murderously thorned *ronce* that still borders every country lane in southern France), cherries, rose hips, mushrooms. There were delicacies—birds' eggs, honey, crayfish, frogs—and snails, both the large Burgundians and the *petit gris* that emerge from their rocky homes after a summer's rain. Perhaps Cro-Magnon learned, as we have, to purge them for several days in a container covered tightly to prevent their departure. He may have used wild garlic to embellish them, but, never having domesticated the bovine race, he lacked butter, the other ingredient needed for a true snail feast.

But beyond these needs of everyday survival, Cro-Magnon man was an artist. He created works of art of magical beauty, and he did so over a period of some 20,000 years, roughly from 28,000 to 8,500 B.C. This is astounding when you consider that the great artistic periods of classic Greece and of the Renaissance each lasted but a few centuries.

These early humans produced bracelets and necklaces made of mammoth's ivory tusks and scallop shells and created little so-called Venus sculptures out of ivory or stone. These finger-sized sculptures, with their exaggerated breasts, buttocks, and sexual organs, have been discovered widely throughout Europe and the Middle East. The best known from the Midi are the Vénus de Lespugue dug up by the count and countess of

St. Périer near Montmaurin (of which the original is in the Museum of Man at the Trocadéro in Paris), the Vénus de Laussel near Sarlat (of which the original is in the Museum of National Antiquities at St. Germain-en-Laye near Paris), the Lady with a Hood from Brassempouy, Landes (also at St. Germain), and the Vénus à la Corne (in the Aquitainian Museum at Bordeaux). We went to the Museum of Man in January 1990 to see the lovely little Vénus de Lespugue but

Lady with a Hood, Brassempouy, 22,000 B.C.
(Photo: Museum of National Antiquities, St. Germain-en-Laye)

Lascaux Cave Painting, Pregnant Animals
(Photo: Maison de la France)

found her sadly neglected. Her roommate in the exhibition case, the Venus of Wissendorf, in Lower Austria, had toppled over and was lying on her back like a dead canary in its cage. These oldest Venuses deserve better treatment.

THE CAVE PAINTINGS

But Cro-Magnon's most exciting artistic expression is the cave paintings. From 28,000 B.C. on, the last of the European glaciers, the Würm (corresponding to the Wisconsin Glacier, most recent of the North American ice ages), filled the valleys and chased Cro-Magnon man upward to the mouths of the limestone caverns. Deep within these caves, lighted by torches, they worked with chisel and bear grease paints to depict the horse, mammoth, bison, and reindeer that nourished them and shared their lives.

Many of these bison and other animals are shown heavy with young, as if to say "May your tribe increase!" Perhaps there is some connection between these pregnant animals and the little maternal Venus sculptures, on the one hand, and the absence of war themes in Cro-Magnon art, on the other. Perhaps the Cro-Magnon culture achieved a peaceful harmony between a nature-related, life-giving Woman and a gentle hunter-fisher Man. Riane Eisler in *The Chalice and the Blade* suggests a correspondence between Cro-Magnon and twelfth-century Midi society, which incorporated "the troubadour view of woman as powerful and honored rather than dominated and despised, and of man as honorable and gentle rather than dominating and brutal" and the principles of the Cathars, who numbered women among their religious and social leaders and abhorred violence.*

A good introduction to the cave paintings can be had at the National Museum of Prehistory, a twelfth-century castle set into the cliff at Les Eyzies. It contains tools and skeletons, a room devoted to the different periods of prehistory, rooms of archaeological discoveries, and reproductions of the cave art. At its entrance stands a huge statue by Paul Darde entitled *Primitive Man*, a hunched-over brute of a figure that does a grave injustice to M. Cro-Magnon, our look-alike.

Cave art had been found at Altamira in Spain in 1879. Near Les Eyzies, it was discovered at La Mouthe in 1895, at Combarelles and Font de Gaume in 1901, and at Cap Blanc in 1911. But the most famous painted cave is at Lascaux on the Vézère, a dozen miles north of Les Eyzies. There, in 1940, four teenagers saw their frolicking dog Robot disappear down a hole. Following him, they found themselves in a cavern the

---

* Riane Eisler, *The Chalice and the Blade* (San Francisco: Harper and Row, 1987), p. 139.

size of a football field, its walls covered with red and yellow ponies, deer, and bison. Their schoolmaster at once summoned the great authority on cave painting, Abbé Henri Breuil. Breuil examined the find a few days later and pronounced it the "Versailles of prehistory."

There is something haunting about the works of art at Lascaux and a dozen other caves in southwest France. These primitives two hundred centuries ago drew curving lines worthy of a Picasso or a Modigliani. They created pigments that lasted until impious moderns began to disturb them—ocher for yellows, ferrous oxides for reds, manganese for blacks. They engraved with pointed flints, applied paint by blowing through hollow reeds, smeared it on with their fingers, or brushed it on with horsehair.

Lascaux, first opened to the public in 1948, has been closed since 1963 because its million visitors had imported enough bacteria and exhaled enough carbon dioxide to threaten the paintings. Only five visitors a day, specially credentialed experts, are allowed in, and those for just thirty minutes. For the rest of us, in 1983 the government opened a replica of concrete and polyester resin right next to the Lascaux original. Nearby is a prehistoric center with a park containing the live counterparts of the animals in the paintings. The replica accurately duplicates the wonders of the real Lascaux but can never compare to the 20,000-year-old original.

You enter the cave of Lascaux (or its replica) in the vaultlike Hall of the Bulls, a chamber one hundred feet long and thirty feet wide whose walls are covered with paintings of four huge bulls as well as horses, deer, and other animals sporting, frisking, almost stampeding. Their large bodies, with smaller heads and legs, convey a feeling of grace and lightness. The painters achieved perspective by leaving a gap between the animals' bodies and the rear legs farthest from the onlooker.

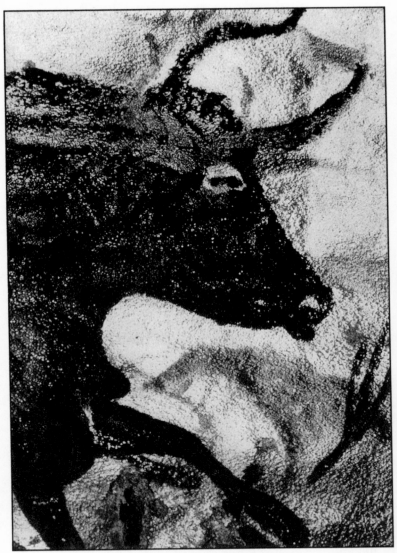

Lascaux Cave Painting, Wild Bull
(Photo: C. Pecha/Maison de la France)

In an alcove off the Hall of the Bulls is the Chinese Horse, its outline accented by a soft black shading and a white underbelly. Above the horse's head, with its short mane, is a geometrical sign, a mystery. Another large room contains a frieze of deer's heads and antlers, streaming along the walls.

With the one and only Lascaux closed, Pech-Merle at Cabrerets, on the Célé, provides the next best combination of great art—spotted horses, bison, mammoth, bear—and ready accessibility. To reach the cave, you drive up the limestone *causse* from the village. On our visit, we enjoyed a delicious lunch of trout fished from the Célé right off the veranda of the Hôtel de la Grotte. Our lunch was enlivened by an occasional surfacing trout and a passing canoe flotilla of topless Amazons.

Before entering the cave, visit the museum, equal to that of Les Eyzies. The film is particularly worthwhile, because in the excitement of the cave, with its spectacularly colored and fluted stalactites and stalagmites, you will have trouble focusing on all the signs of prehistoric man that you will see.

At Pech-Merle, one rock painting or etching is superimposed on another, possibly for lack of space, so that often they are difficult to distinguish. Watch for the red silhouettes of the artists' hands, for the footprints of a woman and child frozen in the mud, and for a giant oak whose roots have burrowed down into the cavern, searching for water.

In addition to the celebrated Lascaux and Pech-Merle, the most exquisite works—all near Les Eyzies—are at Rouffignac, with its engravings, including one of a truly mammoth mammoth, reachable via an underground electric railway; at Cap Blanc, with its bas-reliefs of migrating bison and horses; at Les Combarelles, with engravings of a reindeer herd crossing a river, a lion's head, a bear, giraffes, and antelopes; at Font de Gaume, with colored drawings of deer and bison; and at La

Mouthe, depicting not only ibex and wooly rhinoceros but what looks like an Indian tepee—a tent of animal skins that sometimes served Cro-Magnon as home.

Near Foix, the caverns of Bédeilhac and Niaux have paintings made with bison grease tinted with manganese oxide. At Mas d'Azil, like Lascaux, the parts of the grotto containing the art have been closed to the public, and the remarkable sculpture of the Bristling Horse has been removed to a museum. But one may still see the astounding underground river that runs through the cave, and the huge vault where Protestants sought shelter in the wars of religion.

The cave art breathes mystery. Why are the paintings generally found far inside the grottoes, particularly at Combarelles and La Mouthe? Does this inaccessibility indicate that they had some religious or magical significance, perhaps relating to rites of initiation?

Why, in caves long distances apart, are only animals depicted, with almost nothing of humans, landscapes, abstractions? It seems plausible that there was communication among these primitives, with a few masters setting artistic standards for all. Certainly, shells from the Atlantic and the Mediterranean found near Les Eyzies in the Dordogne reinforce the idea that Cro-Magnons moved around.

Some of the paintings terrify. Why, at Pech-Merle and Font de Gaume, are the animals festooned with white hands and black spots? Why do more than two hundred mutilated hands decorate the walls at Gargas near St. Gaudens? Why does a bison, its entrails trailing, charge a primitive human symbol with a birdlike head in the pit at Lascaux? Why is a weird human figure pierced with lances at Cougnac near Gourdon?

Local priests played important roles in the discovery and interpretation of the cave paintings and other prehistoric archaeology, notably Abbé Breuil of Lascaux, Abbé Durand of Vals, and Abbé Limozi of Pech-Merle. As a young girl, Mary Leakey, who went on to become a leading excavator of the past in Africa, spent the year of 1925 in Cabrerets, near the site of Pech-Merle. She tells of exploring the just-discovered painted cavern with the Abbé Lemozi, a close friend. They had to crawl through narrow passages to find the paintings with their lamps.

Today Pech-Merle's lighting and walkways are excellent, and there is no need to peer or crawl. But be prepared for chill and damp, a small sacrifice to make in these ancient temples. And be sure to arrive early, because visitors are limited to seven hundred daily.

Visiting the Caves

The marvels of the cave concentrated near Les Eyzies on the Vézère are an easy drive on departmental roads from Périgueux (N89, D710, and D49) and Brive-la-Gaillarde (N89, D704, and D706).

On our visit to Les Eyzies, we settled in for three busy days at the Hôtel de Cro-Magnon, an inn charmingly enveloped in Virginia creeper. It was at the height of the August season, and we had no reservations, but the patron managed to find a room for us in his nearby dependency. It was comfortable, and when the shower sprung a leak, he made us accept a substantial discount. At dinner, we celebrated with an entire truffle-in-the-ashes apiece. Also excellent are the Centenaire (E) and Les Glycines.

Our days were spent making the archaeological rounds. First, the excellent National Museum of Prehistory built into the steep rock face a few steps from the hotel. Then, the magically beautiful rock shelters where the first human remains were brought to light—Le Moustier, Laugerie Haute, and La Madeleine across the Vézère. Finally, the cave art itself—Combarelles, Font de Gaume, La Mouthe, Cap Blanc, Rouffignac, and the reproduced Lascaux.

As an alternative to headquartering at Les Eyzies, you could stay at Montignac (Château de Puy Robert [E]); Sarlat (Hostellerie Maysset [E], St. Albert); or Trémolat (Le Vieux Logis). For the great painted cavern of Pech-Merle, we recommend Hôtel de la Grotte or La Pescalerie (E), both on the swift-flowing Célé. For the Cougnac grotto at Gourdon, the Hostellerie de la Bouriane. Further south are the painted caves of Niaux and Bédeilhac south of Foix (Hôtel Audoye-Lons) and Gargas near St. Bertrand-de-Comminges (Hôtel de Comminges; Hostellerie at Sauveterre-de-Comminges [E]; Cedres near St. Gaudens [E]).

This country abounds in rivers ideal for canoeing and kayaking—the Dordogne, Vézère, Lot, Célé, Tarn, and Aveyron. Information can be obtained at the Office Départmental de Tourisme de la Dordogne, 16 rue Wilson, 24000 Périgueux; and Camping Club de France, 6 av. Emilie de Villeneuve, 81100 Castres.

It is possible to participate in archaeological digs for Cro-Magnon relics that are currently being conducted at several points in the limestone country. One such site is close to Cabrerets; information on how to apply for a summer's adventure (for those eighteen and older) is available at the Pech-Merle museum.

Tired of caverns? To the west of Les Eyzies lie the vineyards of Bergerac (Le Cyrano) and Monbazillac (Closerie St. Jacques). Northward are the cities of Brive-la-Gaillarde (Truffe Noir, La Crémaillère) and Périgueux, of Roman towers, Byzantine churches, and splendid cooking (Périgord, L'Oison). To the west, you may discover the medieval towns of Sarlat (La Madeleine, Hostellerie Maysset, La Hoirie), Martel (Voyageurs), and Collonges-la-Rouge (Relais St.

Jacques); the sculptured abbey church of Souillac; Rocamadour with its pilgrimage shrine and unique exhibit of falconry;
the subterranean limestone lake of Padirac (try the Lion d'Or
or Relais Gourmand at nearby Gramat); the Gothic church of
Gourdon (Hostellerie de la Bouriane, Terminus). To the south
flows the Dordogne, boasting the hill town of Domme (Esplanade [E]) and numberless castles (try the Royal Vézère [E] at
Le Bugue or the Château de la Treyne or Pont de l'Ouysse at
tiny LaCave).

The Lot Valley: Gallic Stones

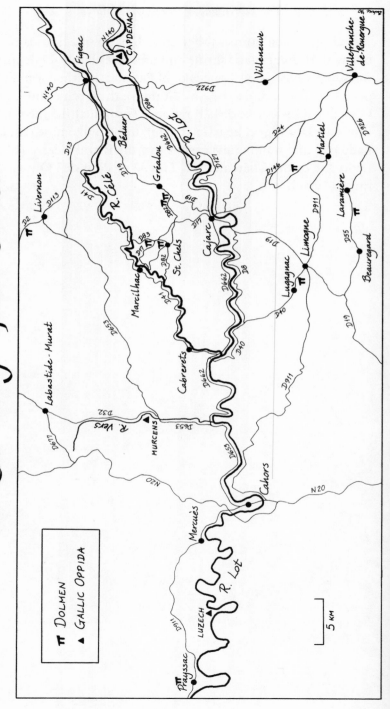

π DOLMEN
▲ GALLIC OPPIDA

5 KM

THREE

The Lot Valley: Gallic Stones

(700 to 51 B.C.)

WHEN the last European glacier thawed in about 7,000 B.C., the era of the cave artists vanished with it. It was seven millennia later before the next great epoch in French history— the blending of the heroic Gauls and their Roman conquerors.

As the glaciers retreated, some of the descendants of Cro-Magnon man must have followed their animal friends to colder lands—the reindeer herds to Lapland, the mammoths to Siberia, the bison to Poland. From Siberia, some early Europeans probably crossed to the Americas.*

---

* Two current theories contest the idea that the first Americans came by way of Siberia. The first, noting that red oxide paint like that in prehistoric tombs in southwest France appeared also in North America (in Maine, Labrador, and Newfoundland), suggests that prehistoric emigration from France across the Atlantic may have occurred as early as 7,000 B.C. A second theory, inspired by recent excavations in Peru and Chile that show signs of human habitation more than 25,000 years ago, revives the long discredited notion that early humans sailed from Asia to South America and then migrated northward.

But some Cro-Magnons must have stayed near their caves and mingled with the new immigrants, Iberian people from the southwest and Ligurians from the east. This French hybrid of the New Stone Age (6,000 to 2,000 B.C.) cultivated crops, domesticated animals, fashioned pottery, wove cloth. He learned to fuse copper and tin into bronze about 2,000 B.C.

In Provence, meanwhile, other immigrants arrived. By 600 B.C. Greek colonists from Asia Minor had established themselves in the Rhône valley and at Marseille.

THE GAULS

Then, from 700 to 500 B.C., hordes of Celts from Bavaria, Bohemia, and central Europe descended on fertile France and swallowed (or were swallowed by) the existing Cro-Magnon mixture. The Romans, observing that these Celts kept fighting roosters (in Latin, "rooster" is *gallus*), called them Gauls.

The French adore their Gallic ancestors. In the delightful comic strip *Asterix*, the little Gallic hero always outwits the block-headed Romans. The Gauls must have looked like today's French from the Midi—of medium height, brown haired, brown eyed—contrary to the idealized French belief that the Gauls were tall, blond, and blue eyed. This belief persists: recently, the nativist politician Le Pen found it necessary to deny publicly that he used a peroxide bleach to produce his blond hair.

The Gauls' speech resembled that of Celts in Brittany, Ireland, Scotland, and Wales. Because they had no written language, little remains save many Celtic place names. Tolosa lives on as Toulouse, Arverni as Auvergne, Cadurci as Cahors. The Celtic suffix *ac*, meaning "belonging to," survives in Figeac, Aurillac, Calvignac, Nérac.

Divided into thirty or more tribes, the Gauls never achieved political unity. Nonetheless, they were adept in battle, skillfully deploying archers, cavalry, and chariots. Under Vercingetorix, chief of the Arveni tribe, they inflicted a defeat on Caesar's legions at Gergovia in Auvergne in 52 B.C. before finally capitulating at Alesia in Burgundy.

Their agriculture stressed growing grain, using fertilizer, rotating crops, and raising sheep, goats, pigs, and cattle. They were also skilled woodcutters. Their industry included pottery, cloth, and baskets. They also knew how to smelt iron, and produced iron weapons and tools for cutting and hammering. In war, in peace, and in art, they were learning to live collectively.

Many of their huts were primitive, reminiscent of those described by another Celt, William Butler Yeats, in *The Lake Isle of Innisfree*, as "of clay and wattles made." Others were more substantial frontier-style log cabins or little stone beehives, prototypes of the *cazels* or shepherd's huts you can see today on the limestone *causses*.

The Gallic religion was distinctive. Gauls worshipped an assortment of gods, elves, and goblins representing their streams and forests. They saw magic in the mistletoe, a parasitic evergreen bush with yellow flowers in winter that is attached by birds to the upper limbs of willows, poplars, maples, mountain ash, and apples. Because it stayed green in winter, mistletoe symbolized the immortality of the soul.

Gallic druids—priests, teachers, and diviners—lived apart, much as did the early Christian hermits of France many centuries later. Seated under their oaks, they dispensed justice and administered herbal remedies made from plants and roots, much as does the French village pharmacist of today. They discovered the curative powers of hot springs.

The Gauls built huge fires on the hilltops to celebrate the summer solstice on June 21, a tradition that survives in today's festival of St. John, held on June 24 to play down its ancient significance. We attended the June 24 fire festival at Cajarc on the Lot, prudently held in the municipal parking lot next to the firehouse rather than on the traditional hilltop. As the flames leapt high, we wondered how many hillside forests had been blackened over the centuries in tribute to St. John. While the town band played "When the Saints Go Marching in," all joined hands in a snake dance around the blaze. It was easy to imagine ourselves amid a pagan ceremony on a wild hilltop twenty-five hundred years ago.

Another memento of Gallic times is the stones that the early French planted on hundreds of uplands beginning around 2,500 B.C., in the New Stone Age, which the Celts, arriving later, adopted as their own. Dolmens—great stone tables with two supports and a top—are the most common, with some four thousand, mostly in Quercy and Rouergue, reported at the last census. Menhirs—large upright stone tablets or monuments—are few, however. The south boasts nothing like the great circle of menhirs at Stonehenge in England or the boulevard alignment at Carnac in Brittany; nevertheless, it does have some one hundred and fifty stone statue menhirs, such as the three-foot-high fertility goddess of Capdenac (in the museum at Cahors) and the larger statues found at Montels (now in the St. Raymond Museum at Toulouse) and in Aveyron (in the Fenaille Museum at Rodez).

Building the dolmens was like a junior version of Egyptian pyramid building. The stones had to be horsed from their nearby quarries on rolling beds of logs, pulled by a score of strong men. Getting the tabletop in place involved covering the site with a tumulus of large gravel to form a ramp. The Egyptian pyramid builders and the dolmen engineers were achieving their constructions at about the same time.

What do the dolmens signify? They could have been altars

or places of sacrifice, but most likely, from the remains found, they were burial grounds.

A dolmen almost one hundred feet long, the largest in the Midi, at Les Fades near Pepieux in the Aude department, has three rooms—antechamber, hall, and tomb. Dating from before 2,000 B.C., it was later used as a cemetery in the Iron Age and the Middle Ages.

The dolmen of Lamalou at Rouet, fifteen miles north of Montpellier, is covered by a vast tumulus some thirty feet long made of small round stones. Bones of more than one hundred people have been removed from the tomb, as well as flint ornaments, weapons, and utensils.

While many dolmens have fallen victim over the millennia to agricultural expansion or to vandalism, they are now protected by the law of 15 July 1980.

The people of the Midi regard the dolmens with reverence, as part of their patrimony. Sometimes, myths survive. Near Livernon, the Martine stone frequently appears decked with flowers, a practice said to ward off fevers. Another fever stone stands at the entrance steps to the great Cathedral of Notre Dame at Le Puy. At Costreaste near Gourdon, the dolmen is known as the Washing Place of the Fairies.

Other large rocks revered by the early Gauls have been treated to what modern preservationists call adaptive reuse. At Vals, near Palmiers and Foix, a medieval church has been built on top of two prehistoric megaliths.

Dolmen chasing can be an exciting sport. Try a loaf of bread, a jug of wine, and a dolmen in the wilderness.

THE GALLIC OPPIDA

Perhaps the most interesting relics of the Gauls are their oppida—stone fortresses located on natural defenses such as steep cliffs, rivers' meanders, and promontories, and reinforced with stout stone walls, moats, and towers. Five of them, near Béziers, Aix, Nîmes, and Marseille, on the Mediterranean, and Uxellodunum, on the Lot, give the traveler today a fascinating archaeological experience.

Greeks from Asia Minor established the first settlement at Ensérune, ten miles southwest of Béziers, in the sixth century B.C. and were absorbed around 300 B.C. by newly arrived Celts. The settlement had been abandoned when the Romans arrived with their first permanent colonization at Narbonne in 118 B.C. The colonists revived it with sewers and pavements but finally abandoned it in the first century A.D.

You can see the Ensérune hilltop, protected by ramparts, and its stone houses with cisterns to collect water, silos to preserve grain, and large ground containers (dolia) to store

Dolmen of the Martine Stone, Livernon
(Photo: Dortes/Giraudon)

Ensérune Dwelling, sixth century B.C.
(Photo: Musée Archéologique, Ensérune)

provisions. The dead were incinerated, and the funerary urns kept in a large necropolis.

An excellent museum on the site contains excavated Greek, Iberian, Etruscan, Celtic, and Roman pottery. From an overlook, you can see from the Cévennes to the Pyrénées. Immediately below is the wetland of Montady, drained in 1247 to make farmland.

Entremont, a mile and a half north of Aix on a steep hill surrounded by ramparts, was the capital city of the Ligurians and Celts of Provence in the third century B.C. In 124 B.C., the first of the Roman legions to invade Gaul overwhelmed the town and enslaved the inhabitants. The legionaries then pitched camp at the nearby hot springs of Aquae Sextiae, which later grew into the city of Aix.

Continuing excavations enliven a visit. Gridiron street patterns position houses made of stone and adobe. The Granet museum in Aix houses statues dug up at the Entremont site.

One of them, a figure of a squatting warrior holding on his knees what appears to be the severed head of a fallen foe, suggests that life for the Liguro-Celts was nasty, brutish, and short.

The site commands a view of Mont Ste. Victoire, the subject of some sixty paintings by Paul Cézanne, Aix's most illustrious son. Looking at the mountain, you can understand Cézanne's passion to capture its massive mountain flanks in strokes of color.

A third oppidum is Nage, situated on a hilltop six miles southwest of Nîmes. The houses, surrounded by walls with towers and gates, are arranged in a grid pattern on the slope. They are simple and straightforward: one square room, with a hearth for cooking in the center. The only amenity is a small temple. The museum in the nearby *mairie* contains pottery, metal work, and weapons found at the site.

A fourth oppidum, St. Blaise, on steep cliffs near the huge Berre salt lagoon fifteen miles northwest of Marseille, has a multiethnic history. Etruscan sailors are thought to have founded the walled hill fortress in the seventh century B.C., exchanging their Italian wine for the local salt. A fire in the fifth century B.C. destroyed the town, and Greek colonists from Marseille took over the ruins in the third century B.C., building houses with several rooms on a gridiron street pattern. Next, the Romans, following their conquest of Marseille in 125 B.C., apparently invaded the settlement, then quickly abandoned it. After the collapse of the Roman empire, the settlement was repopulated by the survivors. Finally, in 1390, medieval robber barons sacked the town, and it was never resettled.

A museum in the nearby abandoned salt customs office houses objects excavated at the St. Blaise site—Etruscan oil jars, Greek vases, and medieval tools and utensils.

Historically, the most important Gallic oppidum of all is

Uxellodunum. After the first Roman fight in Gaul, at Marseille in 125 B.C., and after the first Roman colony, at Narbonne in 118 B.C., the Gauls remained quiescent but unconquered for sixty years. Rome was well pleased with her invasion of Gaul: it secured the military route between Italy and Spain and provided land for retired veterans of the Roman legions.

It was when Caesar took command of the Roman forces that the Gallic Wars (59 to 51 B.C.) began in earnest. With the defeat of the young Gallic chief Vercingetorix at Alesia in 52 B.C., Caesar determined to wipe out the last center of organized resistance in Gaul, the oppidum of Uxellodunum. In 51 B.C., 30,000 Roman legionaries laid siege to the fortress, which was defended by 3,000 Gauls.

Caesar tells the story in his *Gallic Wars*:*

In Caesar's view, although the numbers engaged in this revolt were insignificant, the obstinacy they were showing called for the severest punishment. Otherwise he was afraid that the Gauls as a whole might begin to think that their failure to stand up to Rome had been due not so much to lack of strength as to lack of perseverance, and that the other states might follow the example of Uxellodunum and, making use of whatever strong positions they possessed, attempt to regain their liberty....

Everyone was surprised when Caesar appeared in front of Uxellodunum.... The hill on which the town stood, with its steep precipices, was almost entirely surrounded by a deep valley along which flowed a river.

Caesar goes on to describe how his archers were able easily

---

* Rex Warner, translator, *War Commentaries of Caesar* (New York: Mentor Books, 1987), pp. 200–203.

to keep the defenders from descending to the river for their water, thus leaving them with only one source:

> This was a spot just under the town wall on that side where, for about three hundred feet, there was a gap in the circuit made by the river. Here a spring gushed out of the ground and gave an ample supply of water. Everyone wanted to cut off the townspeople from this spring, but only Caesar saw how it could be done.

First, Caesar built a wooden tower ten stories high so as to command the spring. But the Gauls set it afire. Caesar, however, had ordered his engineers to dig a secret tunnel and divert the spring:

> Finally, our tunnels reached the sources of the spring, which were then tapped and diverted; the spring, which had never failed before, suddenly became dry and the townspeople now lost all hope of deliverance. Yielding to necessity, they surrendered.

And now the bloody end:

> Caesar was aware that his clemency was known to everyone and had no fear that, if he did take severe measures, anyone would think that there was any cruelty in his character. He therefore decided to make an example of the inhabitants of Uxellodunum in order to deter the rest. All who had borne arms had their hands cut off and were then let go, so that as many as possible could see the punishment that had fallen on evildoers.

Despite Caesar's cruelties, he remains a great favorite with many Frenchmen. Napoléon III was a Caesar buff and, in 1865, wrote the massive, two-volume *History of Julius Caesar*. And Voltaire observed that every city in France "competes with its neighbor for the honor of having been the first to which Caesar gave a flogging. We quarrel over what route he used to come and slit our throats, make love to our wives and daughters, and steal our tiny savings."

But where *is* Uxellodunum? The question remains unanswered to this day. There are just too many claimants that roughly satisfy Caesar's description of a high promontory, surrounded on three sides by a meandering river, and with a spring near a 300-foot isthmus. Jean Fantangié, the columnist for the *Dépêche du Midi* already mentioned, recalled in a 1975 piece for that Toulouse newspaper the interminable discussions at the Midi Archaeological Society as to which was the real Uxellodunum:

> M. Carle, Mayor of Luzech, claimed the site for his city, amiably but firmly. Another convinced one, School Inspector Heride, came down strongly for Puy d'Issolud, largely on the strength of Napoléon III's recommendation. M. Maureille, now deceased, shouted his conviction that the true site was Murcens. As for Professor Cour, he was a partisan of Capdenac, reinforcing his point with a lengthy epic verse that proved him a poet of sublime endowment. Finally, the discussion grew so acerbic that, agreement between the skirmishers being clearly impossible, it was unanimously decided to speak no more of Uxellodunum.

Fascinated by this historical treasure hunt, we visited Luzech, Murcens, and Capdenac on the Lot, as well as Puy d'Issolud near Martel on the Dordogne and Uzerche on the Vézère, a site supported by no less than Karl Baedeker in the 1914 edition of his guide to southern France. All these are interesting—Luzech for its Gallic oppidum, the Impernal, its medieval tower, and the neighboring Cahors wine cooperative

Gallic Spring, Capdenac

at Parnac; Puy d'Issolud for its splendid view of the Dordogne valley; the oppidum at Murcens on the Vers near Cahors, with its brave little museum consisting of a few bits of pottery in a wayside shelter; Uzerche for its ancient houses.

But Capdenac, we believe, has the inside track. Its claim is supported by nearby Figeac's native son Jean François Champollion (1790–1832), the Egyptologist who deciphered the Rosetta Stone for Napoléon.

The site itself, largely restored since 1980, certainly fits Caesar's description. The Capdenac promontory is surrounded on three sides by a giant meander of the Lot, the base of the fortress wall on the isthmus, exactly 300 feet as we paced it off, still stands, the probable foundations of the wood tower were uncovered by some recent road building, and, most significant of all, there is on display a cut-off Gallic spring, the Roman underground trench that did the cutting, and the new well built by the Romans from the diverted source. Gazing at all this fascinating hydrology, we heard the beautiful trilling of a nightingale in the wood above.

The people of Capdenac are proud of their Gallic heritage and have named the town square Place Lucter after Lucterus, the Gallic leader of the outnumbered defenders of Uxellodunum. In the square an attractive museum housed in a thirteenth-century dungeon contains a model of a small granite pre-Celtic goddess-mother. (The original is in the municipal museum at Cahors.) Her eyes bulge, her nose is square, her mouth rectangular.

It is worth the effort to climb the 130 steps down the side of the south cliff over the Lot to see what is variously called the "English Fountain" and "Caesar's Spring," thought by the historians of Capdenac to have been built by Caesar to assure his victorious legions a steady water supply. A flick of the light switch at the entry illuminates two basins of limpid water fed from a spring within the rock.

Equally uncertain is the location of another famous Gallic oppidum—Gergovia, capital of the Averni—where, in 52 B.C., young Vercingetorix defeated the Roman legions besieging his forces and almost captured Caesar. A few months later, Vercingetorix was himself defeated at Alesia, in Burgundy, and surrendered to Caesar. After exhibiting his captive for years as a symbol of triumph, Caesar had him executed.

A hill site just south of Clermont-Ferrand claiming to be Gergovia was visited in 1862 by Emperor Napoléon III, who proclaimed it the real thing. It has ever since been a mecca for tourists, but most archaeologists remain unconvinced, placing Gergovia instead to the north of Clermont-Ferrand.

Visiting the Lot Valley

You can make your own search for the authentic Uxellodunum by following the meanders of the Lot upstream for sixty miles or so. Starting at Villeneuve-sur-Lot (La Toque Blanche [E]) on the western boundary of ancient Quercy, today the Lot Department, you can take departmental roads on the north bank of the river clear up to the eastern boundary at Capdenac (Hôtel des Carmes in Figeac), our nominee for the real Uxellodunum. For most of the route, you drive on pavement laid on the old Roman east-west route.

You could vary your standard of living as you work your way east. You might splurge the first night at the luxurious and historic Château de Mercuès west of Cahors, once the palace of the archbishops of Cahors (E).

The second night, you might settle down at the recently refurbished Hôtel Terminus near the Cahors station, with its excellent nouvelle cuisine, or at the bourgeois, comfortable Beau Rivage at Laroque-des-Arcs just east of Cahors, dining deliciously at the riverside restaurant (both establishments are moderately priced). Other good restaurants are La Taverne in Cahors, Marco in La Magdelaine, and Gindreau at St. Medard-Catus.

The third night, try to get one of the two charming bedrooms at the *chambres d'hôte* of Michel and Josi Grouzelle at Montbrun (inexpensive) and sample the variety of foies gras dishes at their restaurant, La Ferme.

Montbrun Château (Photo: John Oakes)

As you dine on the terrace of La Ferme, you can see across the valley of the Lot the steep limestone cliff known as the Saut de la Mounine (Leap of the She-Ape). According to local legend, an early lord of Montbrun, angered by his daughter's love for the son of his enemy, the count of Salvagnac, ordered his men to throw her from the highest cliff. A monk, overcome with horror at the sentence, substituted the count's pet she-ape (*mounine*) dressed in the girl's clothing and hurled it from the cliff. The father, seeing the falling body, was seized by remorse.

Such was his relief when he discovered the substitution of the she-ape for his daughter that he gave the couple a substantial dowry and a proper wedding at the church. The cliff is a popular picnic spot for the people of the canton to this day.

Along your Gallic route, you might detour to take in a few dolmens of the early Gauls—near Prayssac, Livernon, Limogne, Gréalou, St. Chels, Beauregard, and Gramat, all inland from the Lot. They are usually identified by roadside signs, and the detailed Michelin maps indicate many. The huge dolmen at Les Fades can be reached by traveling west on the D610 from Carcassonne to Olonzac, then on the D52 to Pepieux.

At Luzech, do as we did—confer with the local historians at the *syndicat d'initiative* and hear their arguments in favor of their rocky promontory, the Impernal, as the true Uxellodunum. On the heights are indeed traces of a Gallic oppidum, but somehow the site doesn't quite fit Caesar's description. Neither does Murcens, upstream on the Vers. Only Capdenac (Hôtel des Carmes in Figeac), our own contender, seems to match Caesar's scenario. The final verdict is not yet in: every visitor still has a chance, by some new insight, to make history.

There are also Roman vestiges along the route. In Cahors, the Arch of Diana still stands, as do parts of the theater. Upriver, at Vers, you can see traces of the Roman aqueduct that once brought Cahors its water supply.

Being on a Gaul-oriented trip does not require you to close your eyes to other sights along the route. Bonaguil is one of the best preserved of the medieval fortresses. The wine cooperative at Parnac provides a laboratory example of how cooperative marketing can succeed. It has enabled the black-red Cahors wine to regain a standing in the last generation that it has not enjoyed since the Hundred Years' War. Cahors itself has a splendid cathedral and cloister, blocks of picturesque medieval houses along its rue Nationale, and a good little museum, currently being refurbished, of everything from pre-history to the Resistance. Medieval Figeac, and the *bastide* of Villefranche-de-Rouergue (with a good restaurant—L'Univers), also merit a visit.

FOUR

Roman Gaul

(51 B.C. to 410 A.D.)

THE Romans brought to conquered Gaul Roman law and administration; Roman construction and technology; Roman public buildings, roads, aqueducts, and bridges; the Roman language; and the Roman religion as it passed from the old gods to Christianity. Above all, they brought peace, at least three centuries of it. It is no wonder that the conquered Gauls embraced and absorbed their Roman conquerors. Together, they built cities, with forums and basilicas, temples and triumphal arches, houses and baths, theaters and stadia. Together, they venerated Mother Earth in their country villas.

France, adrift since the cave painters, was enjoying her second golden age. To be sure, as the rich grew richer and the great mass of the people found itself sharing less and less in the prosperity of the Roman Empire, the seeds of destruction were being sown. But, while it lasted, the Gallo-Romans, as the historian Gibbon observed, celebrated "the beautiful face of the country, cultivated and adorned like an immense gar-

Maison Carrée in Nîmes
(Photo: French Government Tourist Office)

den; and the long festival of peace...delivered from the apprehension of future danger."*

THE "ROMAN TRIANGLE" OF PROVENCE

Miraculously, the glories that were Rome are preserved today in Provence in a little triangle, forty miles to a side, in a profusion and perfection unequaled anywhere else. How these structures have survived the stealers of stones for close to two thousand years is a mystery, but there they are, telling us how the Roman Empire must once have looked.

Far from being almost unknown, as is so much we write about, the Roman relics of Provence are world famous, much visited, and endlessly described. So we content ourselves with

---

* Edward Gibbon, *The History of the Decline and Fall of the Roman Empire* (London: J.S. Virtue), vol. 1, ch. 2.)

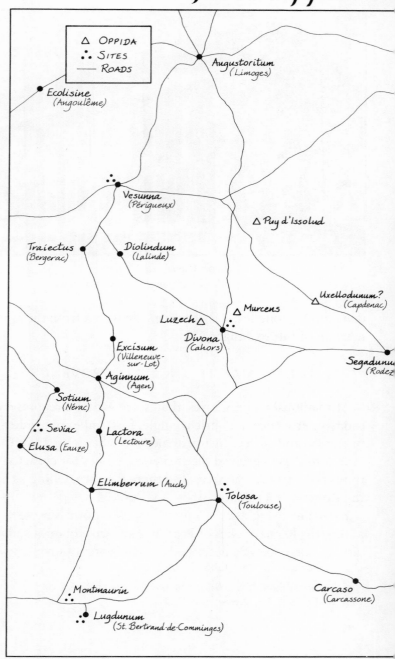

Gallic Oppida,

△ Oppida
∴ Sites
— Roads

Ecolisine
(Angoulême)

Augustoritum
(Limoges)

Vesunna
(Périgueux)

△ Puy d'Issolud

Traiectus
(Bergerac)

Diolindum
(Lalinde)

Luzech △

△ Murcens

Uxellodunum?
(Capdenac)
△

Excisum
(Villeneuve-
sur-Lot)

Divona
(Cahors)

Segadunu
(Rodez

Aginnum
(Agen)

Sotium
(Nérac)

∴ Seviac

Elusa (Eauze)

Lactora
(Lectoure)

Elimberrum (Auch)

Tolosa
(Toulouse)

Montmaurin

Carcaso
(Carcassone)

Lugdunum
(St. Bertrand-de-Comminges)

n Roads and Sites

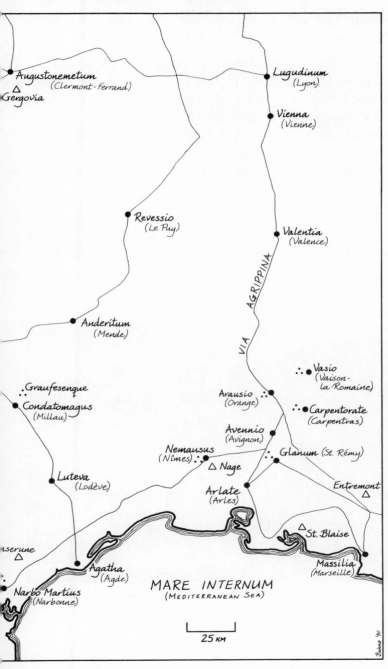

Augustonemetum
(Clermont-Ferrand)
△ Gergovia

Lugudinum
(Lyon)

Vienna
(Vienne)

Revessio
(Le Puy)

Valentia
(Valence)

Anderitum
(Mende)

VIA AGRIPPINA

Vasio
(Vaison-
la-Romaine)

Graufesenque
Condatomagus
(Millau)

Arausio
(Orange)

Carpentorate
(Carpentras)

Avennio
(Avignon)

Nemausus
(Nîmes)   Glanum (St. Rémy)

△ Nage

Luteva
(Lodève)

Entremont
△

Arlate
(Arles)

St. Blaise
△

Enserune
△

Agatha
(Agde)

MARE INTERNUM
(MEDITERRANEAN SEA)

Massilia
(Marseille)

Narbo Martius
(Narbonne)

|—————|
25 KM

Bohm '90

little more than naming the great sites, all within a short drive of Avignon:

- Nîmes (Nemausus), settled by veterans of the Roman legions, with its perfectly preserved Maison Carrée (Square House, an odd name for a rectangular temple 85 by 49 feet), a human-scale model for many a ponderous building for two thousand years; its arena, the scene of gladiatorial combat until Christianity outlawed it in 404; and its Garden of the Fountain, a lovely modern pleasure ground surrounding the ancient spring of Nemausus.

- Pont du Gard, fifteen miles northeast of Nîmes, an intact aqueduct of three arched tiers of golden stone over the river Gardon that brings Nîmes its water supply from thirty-one miles away.

- Orange (Arausio), with its theater, the best preserved in the

Arena, Nîmes (Photo: Thierry/Maison de la France)

Pont du Gard (Photo: Lejeune/Maison de la France)

empire and acoustically perfect; and Arch of Triumph, decorated with scenes of Roman military victories.

- Vaison-la-Romaine (Vasio Vocontiorum), where diggings in the modern town are steadily unearthing the Roman city of the early Christian era, containing luxurious villas of the patricians, with lavish atriums and private baths. The museum exhibits busts and statues in beautiful white marble.

- Carpentras (Carpentorate), with its arches showing Gallic prisoners in chains.

- St. Rémy-de-Provence, a market-garden town, with its nearby Mausoleum, a monument probably to the memory of the Emperor Augustus's grandsons; its Arch, depicting dejected male and female prisoners of war; and the houses, forum, baths, temples, and other remains of the city of Glanum.

- Arles (Arelate), full of Roman relics of the early Christian era—the arena, as large and almost as well preserved as that

Emperor Domitian, Vaison-la-Romaine
(Photo: Thierry/Maison de la France

Arena, Arles (Photo: Thierry/Maison de la France)

at Nîmes; the theater; the Baths of La Trouille; and the Alyscamps, a vast Roman and early Christian necropolis, one of the two hundred scenes of Arles painted by Vincent Van Gogh during his time there in 1888–89.

ROMAN REMAINS IN PÉRIGORD, QUERCY, AND LANGUEDOC

Compared to the Roman marvels of Provence, the Roman remains of Périgord, Quercy, and Languedoc are more modest, best seen as incidents to travels proposed in other chapters of this book.

Cahors (Divona), which sold wine and linen to Rome, has its Fountain of Divona (now Fontaine de Chartreuse), goddess of the spring, across the Lot River; its fragment of a theater in the foundation of the House of Agriculture near the railway station; its nearby arch of Diana with its baths; and its relics of a twenty-mile-long aqueduct bringing water from the Vers River.

Périgueux (Vesona) has its tower of Vesona, an amphitheater, and a Roman wall. The tower, its walls seven feet thick, was erected in the reign of Hadrian (117–138 A.D.) to honor the city's patron goddess. Its architecture is as much Celtic as Roman.

The Romanesque church of St. Just at Valcabres contains a Roman tomb, and the church itself was probably built of stones from the nearby Roman ruins of Lugdunum Convenarum at St. Bertrand-de-Comminges, where a schoolmaster, Gaston Sapène, started the still unfinished excavations in 1926. Built in the early years of the Christian era, Lugdunum had 60,000 inhabitants. Herod, tetrarch of Galilee, fled here after the murder of John the Baptist. Largely destroyed by the Vandals in 468 A.D., Lugdunum boasts impressive diggings,

Arch of Diana, Cahors (Photo: Delvert/Maison de la France)

Tower of Vesona, Périgueux
(Photo: Veguier/Maison de la France)

including its aqueduct, baths, theater, temple, basilica, and forum.

Toulouse (Tolosa) was a major Roman city. Large sections of its Roman brick wall still surround the inner city, but centuries of barbarian invasion have obliterated most of the rest of Roman Toulouse. We shall know shortly how much now lies under the rubble, however: the new Toulouse subway, scheduled for completion in 1992, is almost sure to uncover a Roman forum.

Narbonne (Narbo Martius), founded in 118 B.C., was the

first Roman capital of Gaul. The fine archaeological museum in the old archbishop's palace contains some splendid stones from the Roman past. These were mostly dug from the old fortification walls, where the Barbarians had discarded them, and from the subsoil of the railroad station.

There is much to suggest that early Narbonne was a wine center, as it is today. On a marble sarcophagus, cupids are busy picking and pressing grapes. Drunken Silenus thunders along in his two-horse chariot, a clear case of driving under the influence.

Many of the stones are beautiful: the head of a Roman lady with a swarming-bee hairdo; a superb floor mosaic; the goddess Attis in her Phrygian cap, later appropriated by the Revolution; bullshead altars to the goddess Cybele like those at Lectoure.

The lapidary museum in the deconsecrated Gothic church of Lamourguier contains some thirteen hundred Roman tombstones. Though this may seem an overwhelming number, studying the inscriptions yields many insights into the trades of Roman Narbonne—a juggler, a baker, a roast-meat vendor.

One intact relic is the horreum, a vast underground warehouse that underlay the Roman market. Discovered in 1935, the horreum displays row after row of cubicles for the storage of goods passing through the port.

In 1982, Rome recognized her daughter Narbo Martius with the presentation of a replica of the famous statue depicting the she-wolf suckling Romulus and Remus.

Graufesenque, near Millau (Condatomagus), produced Gallo-Roman pottery of a high order. Vases and urns from its reddish clay have been found all over the Roman Empire, from Britain to the gates of India. You can visit the Graufesenque pottery works, which once employed five hundred workers at its kilns, just across the Tarn from Millau. Specimens of the pottery may be seen in the museums of Millau and Rodez. Another large Roman pottery was located at Banassac, on the Lot below Mende.

ROMAN GARDEN-VILLAS IN GASCONY

Roman remnants in southern France that will particularly delight the traveler are two recently uncovered Roman garden-villas in Gascony. They show how a country gentleman of the Empire lived in the fourth century A.D.

At Montmaurin, in the valley of the Save, the heirs of a Roman squire named Nepotianus built a marble villa of two hundred rooms, occupying ten acres, arranged in a semicircle and fronted by a series of garden enclosures. The structure was completed in the fourth century A.D. and sadly destroyed by the invading Vandals a hundred years later. Excavation started in 1947 and continues today.

The garden-villa at Montmaurin ranks with that at Tivoli east of Rome, Pompeii south of Naples, and Piazza Armerina in Sicily. It commands a splendid view of the snowcapped Pyrénées to the south and the wooded hills of the Little Pyrénées to the east and west. In the entrance courtyard is a six-sided enclosed stone altar. Its Celtic cross appearance, suggests George Foret, the archaeologist who has done the excavating, may have been an attempt to honor the Gallic Tutela and the Roman Venus, thereby pleasing to both the Roman country gentleman and to his Gallic guests. Columns of green-veined marble surround some of the gardens. Nothing is known of the garden plantings, but there is plenty of rich compost for whatever the plantings were. Water from the nearby Save was used lavishly, in a water garden, in a heated swimming pool and baths, and in basins for rearing twenty-two varieties of oysters and other shellfish.

A second notable garden-villa, also of the fourth century A.D., is at Séviac, west of Condom. Though Abbé Mounier, the local priest, discovered three mosaics in a plowed field in 1868, it was not until the 1970s that diggings began in earnest. Great numbers of mosaics have been uncovered, some still in place and others at the museum in nearby Montréal. Their colors are marvelous blues, yellows, whites, grays, reds, and greens. Leaves, flowers, and fruits—the harvest of Gascony—are the motifs. The villa's hot-water heating system would be welcomed in Gascony today. Yet no one knows who built this splendid estate.

Remnants of two other Gascon garden-villas remain. At Valentine, near St. Gaudens, excavation continues on a much smaller villa, with a few columns still erect. And the great garden-villa of Chiraga was once at Martres-Tolosane. It was ornamented by superb busts of a score of emperors and of a

Roman Garden-Villa, Montmaurin, Gascony
(Photo: Marian Schlefer)

Roman Mosaic, Lectoure Museum, Gascony

delightful cherubic baby boy. Sacked by the Vandals in 418 A.D., its buildings were left in rubble. The busts have all been removed to the St. Raymond Museum in Toulouse.

THE ARRIVAL OF THE BARBARIANS

Most Gauls converted eagerly to Christianity, as to all Roman offerings. An exception was the Gauls of the lovely hill city of Lectoure, which we came upon as we drove through Gascony. They remained faithful to the pagan cult of the Great Mother Cybele until the sixth century. One rite involved baptism with the blood of a bull to wash away sins, a pagan concept that may be uncomfortably familiar to Christians "washed in the blood of the lamb." The head of a bull appears on these Gauls' votive stones, twenty of which were dug up in 1540 from beneath the nearby cathedral and can be seen in the museum in the city hall. That the Romans tolerated pagan religions even as they introduced Christianity may help account for the three hundred years of Gallo-Roman peace and prosperity.

From the crumbling of Rome after its brief capture in 413 by Alaric and his Goths to the millennium, the south of France lived in the dark ages. Successive waves of barbarian invaders demolished most of the edifices of Gallo-Roman civilization. There were Alemmani, Vandals, Vascons from Spain (Basques who settled in Gascony), Visigoths (who ruled in Languedoc during the sixth century), and Franks (who settled mainly in the north). In the eighth century, the Saracens arrived from Africa and Spain, stopped only in 732 by Charles Martel at Poitiers. The last invasions, fortunately brief, occurred in the ninth and tenth centuries, when the Vikings seized Bordeaux and sent their beak-prowed, shallow-draft ships up the Lot to Cahors, the Aveyron to Rodez, and the Garonne to Toulouse.

The barbarians from beyond the Rhine and the Danube destroyed much of what they found in southern France. The marble and limestone of the Roman temples, theaters, triumphal arches, and villas were repeatedly vandalized. Roman central government, Roman law, and Roman letters vanished. In their place appeared the local feudal lord in his castle and his vassals in their fields.

But, as the year 1000 passed and the world did not come to an end as the Book of Revelation had prophesied, as the barbarian invaders retreated or became assimilated, and as the church of Rome assumed the mantle of universality that had once adorned the Roman Empire, the Age of Faith dawned. Southern France's ethnic blend of Gaul, Roman, and barbarian was ready for the astonishing creations of the eleventh, twelfth, and thirteenth centuries. The glory of the cave painters and the grandeur of the Gallo-Roman era were to be followed by a third creative age, of religion and poetry and pilgrimage.

Visiting Roman Glories in Provence—and Elsewhere

For the triangle of great Roman sites in Provence, we found ourselves staying at places where the grandeur of the bill approached the grandeur of the sights. For similar splurging, try La Regolido at Fontvielle, Jules César at Arles, Château de Rochegude and Arène at Orange, Imperator Concorde at Nîmes, or Europe and Hiély (restaurant only) at Avignon. More moderate are Domaine d'Enclos at Gordes, Le Castillet des Alpilles at St. Rémy, Emeraude at Uzès, and Le Beffroi at Vaison-la-Romaine.

For a southwesterly look at Gallo-Roman civilization, you might focus on Montmaurin and Séviac (La Gare at Montréal), greatest of the Roman garden-villas, and on the remains of the once great city of Lugdunum Convenorum (now St. Bertrand-de-Comminges), site of Herod's exile. Nearby non-Roman attractions are the archaeological digs at Montmaurin and Aurignac, the church at St. Bertrand, the altars at Lectoure (Hôtel de Bastard), and the cavern of Gargas. Places to stay might be the France at Auch, the Hôtel Comminges at St. Bertrand, or the Cerf Blanc at Aurignac.

Food and lodging at Périgueux and Cahors have been discussed earlier. For Roman Narbonne, try La Résidence, Maphôtel Languedoc and the nearby Relais Val d'Orbieu, and the restaurant Réverbère (E).

FIVE

The Midi: Age of Faith

(1000 to 1300 A.D.)

THE Christian church became the great unifying force of the High Middle Ages (1000 to 1300 A.D.) for many reasons.

The greatest single cause of the church's rise was society's dramatic economic progress after the millennium, much of it itself due to the church. Archbishops and bishops of the cathedrals and abbots of the monasteries had for centuries bought, inherited, and reclaimed vast tracts of arable land. On this land, they fostered every kind of agricultural improvement, even more purposefully than did the secular noblemen on their own estates.

With the end of the barbarian invasions, and the apocalypse foreseen for the millennium averted, farming soon became more than a matter of simply scratching a living from the soil. Forests were cleared, and marshes drained—spectacularly by the great monasteries such as Montmajour and Silvacane in Provence. Better plows were developed, hauled by oxen. Crop rotation—the three-field system—was introduced. The first *pigeonniers* appeared—little stone towers to house pigeons and collect their droppings for use as fertilizer. You can still see *pigeonniers* everywhere in the southwest countryside.

Streams were dammed to make gristmills. Good examples of mills can be found all over—from Marcilhac on the Célé in the Lot to Barbaste on the Gélise in Gascony. Windmills were invented for the same purpose and can be seen today at Castelnaudary on the Canal du Midi, at St. Chels in the Lot, and at Castelnau south of Cahors.

Other inventions eased the rigors of peasant life. Springs were tapped for open-air laundries, such as the one still in use at Varaire on the *causse* of Limogne. Community ovens were opened; those at Collonges-la-Rouge in the Dordogne and at La Couvertoirade in the Hérault are in use to this day.

All this agricultural bustle was made possible by the serfs. They were bound to the land and under the feudal system worked the soil for the benefit of the landowner, whether he was ecclesiastic or secular.

The surplus products of the field entered commerce. Gradually, traders and moneylenders began trade in these commodities with the East and with the northern hinterland. Larger towns came into being, some built on the foundations of Roman strongholds and villas, some new. Fairs soon began to enliven the urban scene.

Another reason for the church's ascendancy in the Age of Faith was the relative weakness of one of its natural competitors for mens' minds: civil government. Civil government was simply no match for the reinvigorated church. The political heirs of the Roman Empire—Clovis and his Frankish Merovingians (about 500 A.D.); the Mayor of the Palace, Charles Martel, who turned back the Saracen invaders in 732; the decadent heirs of Charlemagne; the beginnings of the Capetian dynasty founded by Hugh Capet in 987—all these could offer

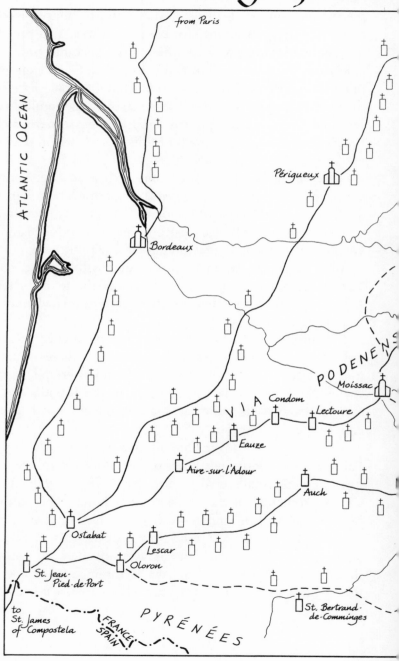

from Paris

ATLANTIC OCEAN

Périgueux

Bordeaux

PODENENS

Moissac

VIA Condom

Lectoure

Eauze

Aire-sur-l'Adour

Auch

Ostabat

Lescar

St. Jean-
Pied-de-Port

Oloron

St. Bertrand-
de-Comminges

to
St. James
of Compostela

FRANCE
SPAIN

PYRÉNÉES

Churches & Pilgrimages

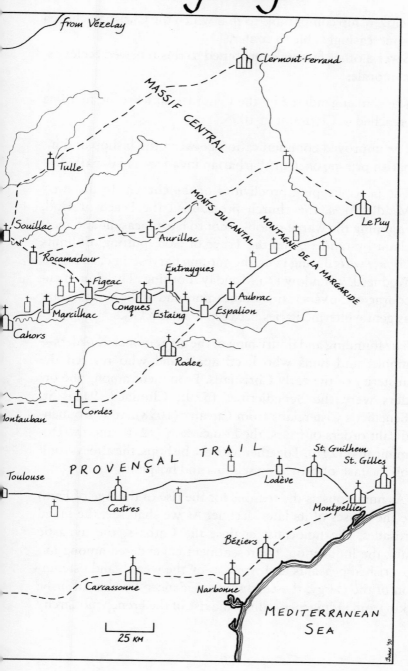

from Vézelay

Clermont-Ferrand

MASSIF CENTRAL

Tulle

MONTS DU CANTAL

MONTAGNE DE LA MARGARIDE

Le Puy

Souillac

Aurillac

Rocamadour

Entraygues

Figeac

Conques

Aubrac

Marcilhac

Estaing

Espalion

Cahors

Rodez

Cordes

Montauban

PROVENÇAL TRAIL

St. Guilhem
St. Gilles

Toulouse

Lodève

Castres

Montpellier

Béziers

Carcassonne

Narbonne

MEDITERRANEAN SEA

25 KM

no citizenship comparable to that which the Christian church was increasingly able to confer.

Several other factors contributed to this renewed ecclesiastical morale:

- The élan engendered by the Crusades, at least the first one preached at Clermont in 1095.

- The improved communication between the bishop and his parish priests, once the barbarian invaders had departed.

- The peace-keeping proclivities of the church. In the early Middle Ages, the church proclaimed the Peace of God, enjoining the warring nobles not to harm peasant and merchant bystanders, and the Truce of God, putting off limits private wars during Lent, the autumn harvest time, and from Wednesday sundown to Monday morning. The church encouraged the veneration of the saints and of the Virgin Mary as gentle intermediaries between man and God.

- The founding and flourishing of the great monastic orders—monks and nuns who lived apart and who revived the austerity of the early Christians. Prominent among the orders were the Benedictines (520), Cluniacs (910), St. Benedict's Cistercians from Citeaux (1098), and two mendicant orders of friars, the Franciscans (1210) and the Dominicans (1216). Together with the bishops, the abbeys took on the task of providing schools and hospitals.

As numerous as the reasons for the rise of the Age of Faith are the causes of its later decline. As we shall see, the failed Crusades, the holocaust against the Cathars, the dynastic wars, the Inquisition, the resentment engendered among impoverished peasants and workers by the wealth and ostentation of the clergy, the corruption evidenced by clerical bribe taking and indulgence selling, the rise of the French monarchy as the claimant for total allegiance, the divisions in the papacy—all combined to bring to an end the wonders of the High Middle Ages.

But for almost three hundred years, the Age of Faith produced a legacy of churches, cathedrals, abbeys, and pilgrimage routes that still awes today's generation of travelers to southern France. With wealthy nobles contributing their treasure and peasants contributing their mites, the church's coffers were able to finance the construction of the south's great cathedrals, country churches, monasteries, and pilgrim hostels.

THE ROMANESQUE CHURCH

In medieval times, four pilgrimage trails crossed southern France, uniting at Puenta de la Reina, in Spain. From there, the trail carried pilgrims on to their goal, the church of St. James (St. Jacques) of Compostella, in western Spain. Along each trail route, like pearls on a string, are the great Romanesque churches built by the monks, peasants, nobles, and townspeople caught up in the religious revival of the eleventh, twelfth, and thirteenth centuries.

The Romanesque church originated in the south because there Latin culture was strongest. Its form derived from the Roman basilica, or law court—a rectangle with two rows of columns holding up the ceiling. It soon took the form of a cross, with its circular apse, behind the altar, facing east to Jerusalem. Its distinction lay in its rounded Roman arches, narrow windows, and massive walls of limestone, sandstone, granite, or brick. Its nave was narrow because its walls could not support too heavy a roof.

The great Romanesque pilgrimage churches—St. Foy at Conques, St. Sernin at Toulouse, St. Trophîme at Arles, St. Gilles near Arles, and St. James of Compostella itself—clearly resemble each other. All five have multiple aisles, long naves (although that of St. Gilles was later shortened by half), and ambulatories surrounding the altar to allow masses of pilgrims to move in organized fashion through the church past the effigies of the saints and martyrs. Off the ambulatories and transepts radiated small chapels for private prayer.

Aside from the special form of the pilgrimage churches, the south's Romanesque often reflected regional differences.

To the west you see Byzantine-style domes, frequently not just one but several. The six-domed St. Front at Périgueux, on the trade route from Byzantium to the Atlantic, so closely resembles St. Mark's in Venice that it may well be derived from it. Cahors's two-domed cathedral is said to have been inspired by an early bishop of Cahors who came from the island of Cyprus. The similarly domed monastery church at Souillac displays some superb Romanesque sculpture of Saints Peter and Benedict, the Virgin, and the Prophet Isaiah.

To the northeast, in the Auvergne, the Cathedral of Notre Dame at Le Puy and the churches at Issoire, St. Nectaire, and Brioude are remarkable for their patterned walls made from the colorful volcanic stone of the region.

To the southeast, in Provence, many of the churches show a strong Roman influence, as in the magnificent carved portals, suggesting triumphal arches, of St. Gilles and of St. Trophîme at Arles. Interiors tend toward monumental austerity, dimly lit by the light filtered through narrow openings.

THE GOTHIC CHURCH

The Gothic church, with its pointed arches, flying buttresses, and stained glass windows, came after 1150 and the heyday of the Romanesque. The buttresses contained the thrust of wide, heavy roofs and of walls with huge stained glass windows, both of which were structurally impossible for the Romanesque. The highly embellished Gothic church, dedicated to Mary, Queen of Heaven, appeared mainly in the north, at St. Denis and Notre Dame in Paris, at Reims, Beauvais, Laon, Amiens, Rouen, and Chartres.

The thousands of churches in the south were, and are, mainly Romanesque. As the medieval monk Raul Glaber wrote, "About three years after the year 1000 the earth had clothed itself in the white robe of the church." By the time the Gothic church arrived around 1150, the south was already magnificently churched and saw no need for many more.

To be sure, the south is not wholly without Gothic churches. Ste. Cecile at Albi and the Jacobins at Toulouse are huge Gothic edifices that were built to fortify and glorify the triumph of the French kings over the Cathars late in the thirteenth century (see chapter 6). Smaller, fortified churches are found in the *bastides* (see chapter 7), new towns built, mainly in the fourteenth century, by the English and French dynasties during their struggle for the soil of France. Gothic churches of the fourteenth-century French Papacy (1304–1379) are at Avignon and old St. Siffren at Carpentras.

Finally, there are a few typically northern Gothic churches built (or grafted onto earlier Romanesque buildings) in the fifteenth and sixteenth centuries. Some of the more important are at Gourdon, Montauban, and Montpezat-de-Quercy in Quercy; at Condom, Auch, and Fleurance in Gascony; at Brive and Tulle in Limousin; at Narbonne in Languedoc; at St. Sauveur in Aix; and at Rodez in Rouergue.

There is a touching story connected with the Gothic cathedral of Notre Dame at Rodez. Started at the end of the thirteenth century, its bell and tower were not completed until 1525. On April 28, 1510, a fourteen-year-old mason's apprentice named Antoine Colinet was repairing the roof of the bell

Narbonne Cathedral (Photo: Narbonne Syndicat d'Initiative)

tower and dreaming of young Adeline, whom he planned to marry. Since he was the last to leave, it was up to him to extinguish the cooking fire lit by the workers. This he did, or thought he did. But during the night the fire rekindled and, fanned by a violent wind, consumed the wooden spire with its covering sheets of lead. Even the bells melted, and the fire and liquid lead rained down on the surrounding houses.

The penitent Antoine swore not to marry until the cathedral's bell tower was rebuilt. The bishop, François d'Estaing, commissioned a splendid replacement bell tower, 270 feet of Gothic lace to be chiselled from the rosy Rouergue sandstone and to be completed in a record fifteen years. Antoine and his fellow masons worked to exhaustion, and the tower was completed on schedule. So it was that on April 28, 1525, in the presence of King Francis I and of the whole town *en fête*, Antoine Colinet, now almost 30, was able to announce his marriage to Adeline. In the summer of 1988, in order "to put Rodez on the map," the townspeople produced a folk play, *Antoine Colinet*, in front of the cathedral. A big hit, it is now done every summer.

Which is more beautiful, the soaring and masterful Gothic or the poetic but earthbound Romanesque? We agree with Henry Adams that it is not necessary to decide. In his *Mont-Saint-Michel and Chartres*, Adams had this to say of the Romanesque church:*

> Men and women who have lived long and are tired—who want rest—who have done with aspirations and ambition—whose life has been a broken arch—feel this repose and self-restraint as they feel nothing else. The quiet strength of these curved lines, the solid support of these heavy columns, the moderate proportions, even the modified lights, the absence of display, of effort, of self-consciousness, satisfy them as no other art does. They come back to it to rest, after a long circle of pilgrimage—the cradle of rest from which their ancestors started.

And of the Gothic:

> The peril of the heavy tower, of the restless vault, of the vagrant buttress; the uncertainty of logic, the inequalities of the syllogism, the irregularities of the mental mirror—all these haunting nightmares of the Church are expressed as strongly by the Gothic cathedral as though it had been the cry of human suffering, and as no emotion had ever been expressed before or is likely to find expression again. The delight of its aspirations is flung up to the sky. The pathos of its self-distrust and anguish of doubt is buried in the earth as its last secret. You can read out of it

---

* Henry Adams, *Mont-Saint-Michel and Chartres* (New York: G.P. Putnam's Sons, 1980), p. 16.

whatever else pleases your youth and confidence; to me, this is all.

THE CLOISTERS

Diocesan cathedrals and parish churches, whether Romanesque or Gothic, were the main structures of the church of Rome; monasteries, on the other hand, were the home for those religious people who wished to live away from the world. Their abbots presided as feudal lords over vast estates. The leading monastic orders had numerous branch houses, or priories. The Cluniac order, headquartered in Burgundy, had some two thousand houses under its sway and maintained a sumptuous palace in Paris, now the Cluny Museum.

Monasteries were built following a practical pattern. In the center was an open, arcaded cloister, usually a flower and herb garden. Here, the monks, friars, or nuns could walk and meditate. On one side, usually the south, was the chapel. The other three sides contained a dormitory, a refectory, and a chapter house where business meetings could be held.

Many a monastery catered to the pilgrims who traveled by. On the pilgrimage trail called the Via Podenensis are the famous houses at Le Puy, Conques, Marcilhac, Cahors, Moissac, and Flaran. On the Provençal pilgrimage trail lie the great abbeys of Montmajour and St. Gilles in the vicinity of Arles and that of St. Guilhem-le-Desert north of Montpellier.

Many other abbeys in the south are well worth visiting as monuments to monkish isolation, industriousness, and power in the Age of Faith: the Cistercian abbeys of Silvacane on the Durance and Sénanque near Gordes in Provence, devoid of any decoration that might distract the monks at prayer; Valmagne near Pézenas; Fontfroide south of Narbonne; Lagrasse south of Carcassonne; St. Martin-du-Canigou and St. Michel-de-

Capital of St. Michel-de-Cuxa
(Photo: French Government Tourist Office)

Cuxa in the Pyrénées near Prades; St. Bertrand-de-Comminges; Carennac, Brantôme, and Cadouin in the Dordogne
region; and La Chaise-Dieu north of Le Puy.

The carved capitals from the cloisters of the two Pyrenean
abbeys, St. Martin and St. Michel, have been largely reassembled at The Cloisters, the Metropolitan Museum of Art's
imposing medieval museum on the Hudson at 190th Street in
New York. This Rockefeller-funded treasure contains parts of
five medieval cloisters and a splendid treasury of tapestries,
ivories, sculpture, stained glass, vessels of precious metal, and
other examples of the wealth of the monastic orders—a wealth
that was later to prove their undoing.

Particularly interesting at The Cloisters are the stone carvers' bestiaries—images of outlandish animals unknown to zoologists. There is the manticore, with a lion's head and a man's body; the basilix with its transfixing stare; the pard, bearded like a tiger; the griffin, with the body of a lion and the wings of an eagle; the centaur; and the two-headed amphisbaena, capable of moving in either direction.

An American embarking for southern France can receive at The Cloisters a glorious preview of the cloistered life as it was actually lived in the twelfth century. The captious may complain of the removal to New York from southern France of all these glories. The curator will patiently reply that the cloister of St. Guilhem was demolished in the Revolution and its capitals scattered; that the Langon chapel was serving as a dance hall; and that the magnificent stone effigy from the Spanish apse, turned on its back, was being used to bridge a brooklet.

THE COMPOSTELLA PILGRIMAGE

The pilgrimages spurred the building of churches and cloisters, just as churches and cloisters, strategically placed every twenty miles or so, made possible the pilgrimages. Whether to Rome for Jesus' sake, to Canterbury for St. Thomas à Becket, or to Compostella for St. James, pilgrims set out for all sorts of reasons—to fulfill a vow, to obtain absolution for some misdeed, to demonstrate faith, as tourists or as substitutes for someone able to hire a proxy. The pilgrim's journey, fulfillment, and return are as old as Moses on the mountain and Jesus in the desert.

Like most pilgrimages, that of St. James is shrouded in myth. The saint, a fisherman on Lake Galilee, followed his master's command to become a fisher of men. After a mission to Spain,

Compostella Pilgrim, Terra Cotta Bust, in Museum,
Flaran Abbey, Gascony

he returned to Jerusalem and was beheaded at Herod's order.
The martyr's body was returned to Spain by ship and buried
in the countryside of Galicia. Lost until the ninth century, the
grave site was rediscovered one starry night by a shepherd.
The name "Campo Stella" refers to this field of stars.

The mud church built on the site of the grave was later
enlarged into the Cathedral of Compostella. According to the
legend, St. James appeared before the aging Charlemagne in a

dream. Pointing to the Milky Way, which would lead the emperor to his body, the saint asked to be delivered from the Saracens. Charlemagne obeyed, waging war against the Saracens, and heroic Roland and the other paladins fell to Basques defending the Pyrenean pass of Roncevalle. Charlemagne ordered their remains brought back to the churches along the Compostella trail, and the story of the defeat became part of the *chansons de geste* of the eleventh century.

Pilgrims to Compostella soon acquired a characteristic costume—large-brimmed hat, cape, mantlet, *bourdon* or staff, a cockleshell (*coquille*)* as a sort of medal, a gourd and mess kit, and a canvas bag for passport and papers. Returned pilgrims became members of an alumni association known as the Confrérie de St. Jacques, later opened to fraternally inclined nonpilgrims. More than fifteen hundred attended a Paris dinner of the Confrérie held on July 25, 1327.

A huge service industry came into being along the Compostella trail to provide for the needs of the pilgrims. Abbeys or hospices exacted no set charge for a night's stay, but gifts were gratefully received.

The walled city of Couvertoirade, south of Millau in the Cévennes, was a marshalling point for the Compostella trail, its interior fields transformed every night into a camping ground for weary travelers. Couvertoirade stands today pretty much as it was in the days of the pilgrimages. Owned first by the Knights Templars, it devolved upon the Knights Hospitaler when the Templars were dissolved and their lands confiscated in 1312 by Philip the Fair.

---

* The cockleshells found on the sands surrounding Mont St. Michel, the great monastery in Brittany, became the symbol of all pilgrimages, particularly that of St. James—hence, *coquille St. Jacques*. Good recipes involve a combination of scallops, mushrooms, shallots, bread crumbs, and white wine.

What was almost an official travel guide appeared in 1130. Commissioned by Pope Calixtus II, the Codex Calistinus, or Book of St. James, was actually written by his chancellor, Aymery de Picaud, and recounted the many miracles attributed to the saint. (A typical one, memorialized in a window of the Cathedral at Tours, concerns a young pilgrim from that city who was hanged. St. James cradled the young man's head on a gibbet for several weeks and returned him alive and well to his family.) The codex also told where lodging and water might be found and described the route of the pilgrimage in detail, providing helpful insights into the habits and mores of the route's inhabitants—usually unfavorable.

The pilgrimages were early exercises in social democracy. Kings and cardinals and dukes, peasants and burghers and strays, traveled together on terms of some equality. The same democratic spirit seems to have governed the building of the churches of that era.

Four principal routes carried the pilgrims through France before they joined in the Pyrénées for the final long walk to Compostella. The Paris route started at the Tour St. Jacques in Paris, following the rue St. Jacques toward Tours, Poitiers, St. Jean d'Angély, Saintes, Bordeaux, and Ostabat. The Vézelay route went through Nevers and Périgueux to join the Paris route at Ostabat for the Pyrenean crossing. The Via Podenensis, starting from Le Puy, and the Provençal route, starting from Arles, will be described in detail below.

THE VIA PODENENSIS

The most famous route of the Compostella trail was the Via Podenensis, used not only by Frenchmen but by thousands from Germany and eastern Europe. From Le Puy in the Auvergne Massif Central, the route wound southwest through the mountain ranges of Velay, Margeride, and Aubrac, where every rocky outcropping potentially concealed a band of brigands. The pilgrims then traversed the high limestone plateaus between the Célé and Lot rivers, where water was scarce, the winter winds cruel, and the summer sun merciless. After Moissac, they entered the gentler land of Gascony. But the forbidding wall of the Pyrénées lay ahead. At the Spanish border, they had come five hundred miles from Le Puy, with the whole north coast of Spain to traverse before they reached the shrine of Compostella.

The exact route of the Via Podenensis survives as Grande Randonnée 65–651 of the French hiking trails, used today for anything from an hour's stroll to a two-month's backpacking adventure. Thirty miles or so that we particularly enjoyed start on the *causse* of Figeac and descend to the Célé river at Marcilhac. Our hike began at a stone farmhouse in whose enclosed yard paced a fierce-looking German shepherd. A painted sign warned us: "Chien Méchant." To our surprise, the "wicked dog" leapt the enclosure, licked our hands, and hiked along with us on the most amiable terms.

We followed the rugged limestone *causse*, sometimes in forest shade along paths hedged by brambles bearing delicious blackberries and murderous thorns, sometimes across barrens covered with scrub oak and dwarf juniper (the same juniper whose berries, transported down the Lot on barges to Bordeaux and there transhipped for delivery to the Low Countries, gave its aroma in the Middle Ages to Holland Gin). Along the way, we saw the obelisk that once marked the limits of the abbot of Figeac's domain, the hill town of Faycelles, the château of Béduer, the cemetery of Gréalou with its ancient cypresses, and a fine dolmen, before we descended to Marcilhac and its ruined abbey on the banks of the Célé.

But let us rejoin the pilgrims at the beginning of their long trek, in Le Puy, a city built on the turrets of extinct volcanoes. It was there in 951 that Bishop Godescalc, one of the first pilgrims to Compostella, decided to make a shrine and a stopping point on the way to Spain. With this decision, pilgrims—and prosperity—came to Le Puy, which continued to thrive until it was undone by the ravages of the anti-Cathar crusade and, later, by the English and Burgundians.

The cathedral of Notre Dame, dating mainly from the first half of the twelfth century, is one of France's Romanesque glories. To reach it, you climb through the old ecclesiastical and feudal town over narrow streets cobbled with lava. Both sides of the approach are lined with shops displaying the delicate wares of the local lace makers. Behind the cathedral looms the fantastic pinnacle of Mt. Corneille, a volcanic rock surmounted by a huge statue of the Virgin cast from melted-down guns taken at Sebastopol in the Crimean War.

The cathedral's facade alternates white sandstone, brick, and black volcanic breccia in almost mosaic designs reminiscent of Spanish-Moorish churches. Rising behind the choir is a beautiful seven-story bell tower. You approach the porch up a series of steep steps, and, as you enter, you pass the fever stone, a dolmen to which were attributed magic powers of healing. Note, too, the wooden doors carved with scenes from the New Testament. Inside them, like all the Romanesque churches of the south, the cathedral is dark, making all the more striking the tiny black Virgin on the high altar, her gold-encrusted red velvet gown and her cape of Le Puy lace almost luminous under the crown of altar lights. She is a copy of the medieval image destroyed during the Revolution.

You exit through the twelfth-century cloister to the north of the choir and pass through the remains of the fortifications that separated the powerful bishopric from the town. The bishops held their powers directly from the Holy See and had

Cathedral of Notre Dame, Le Puy (Photo: Ministère de la Culture et de la Communication)

the right to coin money. They were thus often in conflict with the lords of Polignac, whose ruined feudal château still stands three miles from the city.

One of the chief curiosities of this curious town is the little church of St. Michel d'Aiguilhe, perched on a needle of volcanic rock 260 feet high and reached by a staircase of 271 steps.

The church dates from the end of the tenth century, and the chancel is still older. With its glowing glass, it provides a jeweled setting for holy objects brought back from the pilgrimages.

From Le Puy, the French, German, and Burgundian pilgrims headed west over the volcanic mountains of Velay, the mountains of the Margeride, and the grim and arid plateau of Aubrac. On a dark and stormy July evening, we passed over the Aubrac plain, skirting granite rock masses as big as our car and only occasionally sighting a human habitation. We were on the ancient Roman Via Agrippina. At dusk, we came to Aubrac, described in the codex as "a poor place in a vast solitude."

Legend and truth intertwine at Aubrac. It seems that, as he was returning from Compostella in 1120, a young knight named Alard of Flanders found the severed heads of thirty pilgrims in a brigand cave. Alard took a double vow: to provide hospitality for the pilgrims and to chase the brigands from the Aubrac plain forever. He founded an order, the Dômerie, made up of warrior knights to fight the brigands, monks to serve the religious needs of the pilgrims and to supervise the order's vast farm and timberlands, and religious sisters to cook for the pilgrims, make their beds, and wash their feet. From 1200 to 1215, the order built a church and a great hospice capable of housing five hundred pilgrims.

Toward 1500, when interest in pilgrimages to Compostella diminished, the order became a model farm for the poor and aged. In 1533, Francis I, grateful to the Dômerie for helping to ransom him from his captivity in Spain after the disaster at Pavia, built a forest house nearby for his hunts. That forest house, together with the church and a defensive tower, remains today.

Fire destroyed the Dômerie's main building in 1700. The

final blow was dealt by the Revolution. By Decree of 24 Floréal, Year VI, the old folks were transferred to the town of St. Geniez, and the Dômerie land was sold off in small parcels. But, as mentioned, the church of Notre Dame of the Poor still stands. At first, it seems forbidding in its Romanesque weight and severity, especially at dusk, when we saw it. But this makes all the more touching the wildflowers lying wilted on the altar and the notebooks written by the pilgrim visitors of today.

From Aubrac, the trail forks into two branches. The lesser goes to Moissac via Rodez, Villefranche-de-Rouergue, Villeneuve d'Aveyron, Cordes, and Montauban. The main route descends to the Lot at St. Côme, a fortified town with a tenth-century chapel. It then proceeds downstream to Espalion and the ruins, dating from the tenth through the fifteenth centuries, of the fortress of Calmont d'Olt, where weapons of medieval siege warfare are on view.

Seven miles further down the Lot, you come to Estaing, a town always strongly attached to the illustrious family that gave it its name, to Catholicism, and to memories of the Compostella pilgrimage. The splendid château of the Estaing family, a nunnery since 1836, is the scene of a spectacular son et lumière on July and August weekends.

But the best time to visit is on the first Sunday in July, at noon, when a procession in honor of St. Fleuret, the town's patron saint, starts from the church. We managed to stake out an advantageous post in front of the inn, Aux Armes d'Estaing. With most of the townspeople playing roles or participating as themselves, the procession was highlighted by

- St. James pilgrims, complete with cockleshells, shepherds' staffs, and wine gourds;

- the Penitents, their eyes peering from their hoods;

- St. Michael, scales in hand for weighing souls, St. Peter,

St. John the Baptist and Lamb,
Estaing Procession

bearing the keys to paradise, St. Paul, preaching from his Bible, and St. John the Baptist, barefoot, leading a lamb by a leash;

- bishops, cardinals, and the pope;

- the municipal council, bellies well constrained by tricolor sashes, surrounded by the fire department;

- five hundred years of great d'Estaing ecclesiastics and warriors, from Baron Tristan who rescued the king of France at the Battle of Bovines in 1214, to Bishop François who constructed the marvelous steeple at Rodez's Cathedral, to Admiral Charles Henri who commanded the French fleet off Yorktown and so helped emancipate the United States from England (ten years later, as the representatives of the Revolution strapped him to the guillotine, he is supposed to have suggested to his executioner that his head be sent to the English—"they'll pay you well for it!");

- beautiful little schoolgirls portraying the Holy Family;

- and, last of all, her robe and hair in disarray, Mary Magdalene.

The procession over, we joined the townspeople at the inn for a copious Sunday dinner.

From Estaing, the trail, leaving the Lot, winds through forest laced with bracken to the pilgrimage town of Conques, where, in the eleventh century, Abbot Odobric built the bulk of the Conques church of Ste. Foy, giving it a sense of great architectural unity. St. Sernin in Toulouse and St. James in Compostella are in part modeled after Ste. Foy.

Ste. Foy was a girl of eleven when martyred at Agen, where her bones were kept. According to legend, the monks of Conques, badly needing a tourist attraction, sent one of their number as a mole to the Agen monastery to steal the bones. After six years of duplicity, he made off with the booty one night, to the great glory of Conques.

To house the bones, the monks of Conques built a reliquary golden statue, encrusted over the centuries with gifts of jewels and gold from the pilgrims. You may see it in the treasury today. Its gold head may startle you—it represents what is likely a fifth-century Roman, perhaps an emperor, rather than the youthful saint.

Much more interesting are the church, the cloister, and the old houses of ocher sandstone with roofs of round gray slates

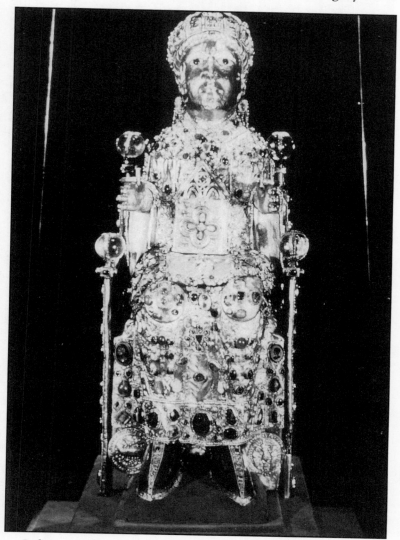

Reliquary of Ste. Foy, Conques (Photo: Maison de la France)

Abbey Church, Conques (Photo: Gaël/Maison de la France)

laid like fish scales. The monastery was wrecked by a Protestant attack in 1561 during the religious wars, and the church was near ruin in the nineteenth century when Prosper Mérimée, inspector-general of historic sites, organized a national campaign to save it. Much of the restoration has occurred since 1974.

The real treasure is the church itself. Its dim nave is lined with arches that reach out in rhythmic progression to cross the aisles and upward to cross the vaults. Indirect light filters down until your eye reaches the crossing of the transept, where direct light falling from the tower dramatically illuminates the high altar. The tympanum has a notable sculpture of the Last Judgment.

To appreciate the simplicity and perfect articulation of the curved and rectilinear masses of Ste. Foy, approach it, as the pilgrims did, over the hills, either crossing the valley to the south or descending from the east. Be sure to lean on the parapet at the roadside to look down on the scalloped roofs of the chapels radiating from the curved roof of the ambulatory, then rising again to the curve of the choir and, above it, to the octagonal tower. If you walk on farther, you can picnic, as we did, on a high bluff overlooking the town and the whole wild valley.

A mile or two to the west of Conques is a tiny chapel dedicated to St. Roch, the patron saint of pilgrims. Born in Montpellier in the fourteenth century, St. Roch, like St. Francis, gave all his property to the poor. According to the legend, on his return from a journey to Italy, he was set upon by outlaws and wounded in the leg. Left for dead in the forest, he was saved from starvation by an amiable dog who every day snatched a loaf of bread from his master's table to bring to the saint. The polychrome statue of him in the chapel shows him in his attire of a Compostella pilgrim, his left stocking down to expose a wound on his knee and, at his side, the little dog with a bun in his mouth.

A side trail then proceeds to Villeneuve in Aveyron, where the bishop of Rodez established a church and monastery in 1069. It was a pilgrim's stop, as affirmed by three wonderful paneled frescoes recently uncovered in the chapel depicting pilgrims in full regalia, and the town was a sanctuary, so designated by stone crosses, three of which may still be seen. The bishop also instituted an animal fair, a not-to-be-missed event that still takes place on the first Monday in July.

The main trail passes through Figeac, whose Benedictine abbey was destroyed in the religious wars, and continues to Marcilhac on the lovely little Célé River. An appealing deaf-mute guide, equipped with a neatly copied multilingual explanation, will show you around the ruins of Marcilhac's eleventh-century Benedictine abbey. The abbey was sacked by the English Free Companies in the Hundred Years' War and finally destroyed during the religious wars. Some of the massive walls still stand, however, and the guide will show you a primitive Romanesque sculpture of the Last Supper and the later flamboyant-Gothic fifteenth-century chapel, still in use.

The pilgrims' next stop was Cahors, built on a rocky peninsula overlooking the Lot River, which is crossed here by the finest fortified medieval bridge in France, the Pont Valentré. The avenue Gambetta separates the new town from the old, with its narrow streets, particularly the rue Nationale, its closely packed ancient houses, and its barbican and walled fortifications.

At the heart of the old town is the cathedral of St. Etienne and its ecclesiastical buildings. The jewel of the cathedral is the north portal with its Romanesque sculptures showing Christ surrounded by figures representing St. Stephen's martyrdom by stoning, the Virgin and the Apostles whirling about, the angels dancing. The sculpture in the cloister is much later and passes from Gothic to Renaissance. On Saturday mornings in summer, the cathedral square is filled with farmers with their *primeurs*—the freshest artichokes and melons, eggplant and plums, tiny string beans and succulent berries.

Continuing our pilgrimage southwestward, we pass Castelnau with its three windmills, Vaserac, and Lunel and come to Moissac. Founded by Benedictines in the seventh century, Moissac reached eminence when the Cluniac order took over in 1017.

The monastery was sacked in the Revolution, but there remains the magnificent carved portal and the cloister.

Prophet Jeremiah, Moissac (Photo: Maison de la France)

The tympanum of the portal depicts the bearded Christ in Majesty sitting in Last Judgment at the Second Coming. He is surrounded, as proclaimed in the Book of Revelation, by four-and-twenty ancients and by the four winged symbols of the Evangelists: Mathew—Man, Mark—Lion, Luke—Ox, and John—Eagle. Remnants of the color that enlivened the walls and sculptures of all Romanesque churches can be seen around the Christ's head.

Beneath the tympanum is a scalloped portal with an extraordinary central pillar adorned by crossed and interlocking lions and the contorted figure of the prophet Jeremiah. The unknown sculptors depict themselves in the doorway, one handling his tools, the other examining his creation.

The carvings in the cloister were done before 1100, fifteen to twenty years earlier than the portal. The evolution is fascinating, from the Gallo-Roman style of the low-relief archaic figures on the corner piers of the cloister to the distortion and dynamism of the carvings of the portal. In the church at Souillac, in the Dordogne, you can see an even more extreme later carving of the prophet Isaiah, his twisting body and sweeping draperies filling the entire jamb.

As you continue south from Moissac over the Garonne into Gascony, the trail crosses an abbey and several ancient bishopric churches.

At Lectoure, below the church is a fountain where pilgrims could quench their thirst. Condom has a late Gothic cloister open to the exterior.

Just south of Condom is the abbey of Flaran, founded by the Cistercians in 1151, ruined in the religious wars, and now being restored by the Gers department. Especially worth seeing are the church, the cloister, and the monks' refectory and dormitory. The abbey, a rest stop on the Compostella trail, contains an excellent trail museum.

Cloister, Flaran Abbey, Gascony

At Aire-sur-l'Adour lies Ste. Quitterie, a fifth-century Visigoth princess, in her marble sarcophagus covered with Biblical scenes such as Jonah and the whale, Daniel in the lion's den, and Adam and Eve.

Thence, the Via Podenensis, soon joined by other branches of the trail, reaches Ostabat, St. Jean Pied de Port, Roncevalle, and Puentas la Reina in Spain, to continue westward to Compostella.

Visiting the Podenensis Trail

You might start where the pilgrims started, at Le Puy (Hôtel Christel or Hôtel Licorn). At Lamastre, you will find excellent food and lodging at the Château d'Urbilhac (E) and Midi (E) or the more modest Négociants.

In the "vast solitude" of Aubrac, consolation is to be found at Grand Hôtel Proyheze (E) at Aumont-Aubrac, Voyageurs-Vayrou at St. Chely d'Aubrac, and at Michel Bras (E) at the ski resort of Laguiole, where the mashed potato reached its apotheosis.

As the trail reaches the Lot River, a good place to spend the night is Espalion (Moderne), Estaing (Aux Armes d'Estaing), or Entraygues (Truyère), or perhaps Conques, where the hospitable inn bears the name of the patron Ste. Foy.

Down the trail and down river, near where the Lot and the Célé have their confluence at Cabrerets, you can choose between the down-to-earth Hôtel de la Grotte, with its restaurant overlooking the Célé, or the superb La Pescalerie, which has its own vegetable garden. Cabrerets might be a good place to change your locomotion from driving to either hiking along the Compostella trail on the high *causse* or floating down the Célé by rented canoe or kayak.

The next night can be spent in Cahors (see chapter 3). If you are pressing on toward Moissac, you might wish at least to dine at Depeyre (E) at Montpezat-de-Quercy or at l'Aubergade (E) near Puymirol, both of them favored by the red Michelin hotel and restaurant guide.

As the trail descends through Gascony, consider the famous Table des Cordeliers at Condom, the Domaine de Bassibe (E) near Aire-sur-l'Adour, or the Ténaréze/Florida at the spa town of Castéra-Verduzan. Here, you could break training either by luxuriating in a mineral bath or by taking in the horse races at the finest track in Gascony.

THE PROVENÇAL TRAIL

The Provençal trail served pilgrims coming south down the Rhône valley and westward from northern Italy and converging at Arles. There, they gathered northeast of Arles at the abbey of Montmajour and its priories and paid their respects to the relics of St. Trophîme in the cathedral at Arles.

Montmajour was founded in the tenth century by Benedictines who began by building a chapel dedicated to St. Pierre that incorporated caves inhabited by a group of hermits guarding the Christian burial ground. The abbey slowly expanded its rule and its wealth by draining the marshlands between the Alpilles mountains and the Rhône. It financed these efforts by selling pardons, an activity that drew up to 150,000 pilgrims at one time. Sold off as junk during the Revolution, it has been patiently restored.

Montmajour's church of Notre Dame, part of the cloister, and the nearby Ste. Croix chapel, all of which we see today, were built in the twelfth century. There is a marvelous rhythm to the arches of the cloister, more complex than the earlier cloisters of St. Trophîme.

As pilgrims approached St. Trophîme, they must have knelt in wonder before the magnificent portal through which they were about to enter. Above them, the Last Judgment, as at Moissac, showed the Christ surrounded by the symbols of the four Evangelists. With angels officiating, those elected for heaven approached from the left, while on the right the condemned were led off to hell. Pilgrims could read from the sculptures of both portal and cloister the events of the Resurrection, the martyrdoms of the saints, the life of St. Trophîme, and the origins of Christianity in Arles.

The next stop on the pilgrimage was St. Gilles, the eastward limit of the possessions of the count of Toulouse, twelve miles west of Arles. St. Gilles's port embarked pilgrims to the Holy Land and carried on a brisk trade with the Orient. Its great fair in September drew merchants from both the Orient and the north of Europe. It is difficult today to imagine the vastness of its monastery in the twelfth century. The abbey church was

St. Gilles, west facade (Photo: Lejeune/Maison de la France)

more than twice its present size, with monastic buildings stretching out to the south and east.

The pilgrim approaching the abbey church would first see the three-arched portico of the abbey. In the style of a Roman triumphal arch, it is embellished with a great frieze recounting Christ's life from Palm Sunday through the Resurrection and beneath, between the pilasters, with extraordinary carvings of the Apostles and saints. These carvings are clearly by different masters and move from a plain antique style to supple and deeply incised, more expressive forms.

Beyond the present church, to the east, lie the ruins of the former chancel with its ambulatory and radiating chapels. The pilgrim would certainly have descended into the crypt to view the tomb of St. Gilles, who achieved sainthood in the eighth century through his benefices to the poor and his miraculous rescue of a hind pursued by a huntsman whose arrow Gilles snatched in midair. Kindness to animals was an appealing saintly trait of Sts. Roch, Gilles, and Francis.

The next stop on the trail was Montpellier. It was a center of spice import, and the merchants, aware of the therapeutic value of spices and perhaps of the writings of Hippocrates, treated the pilgrims' ills. Over the years, these informal medical schools drew more and more students and formed the nucleus of today's great university. Henry James said of Montpellier:

> The wide, fair terrace with its beautiful view, the statue of the grand monarch; the big architectural fountain, which would not surprise one at Rome, but does surprise one at Montpellier; and to complete the effect, the extraordinary aqueduct, charmingly foreshortened—all this is worthy of a capital, or a little court-city.*

The pilgrims stopped also at the abbey of St. Guilhem-le-Desert on the Hérault River northwest of Montpellier. The abbey got its name from one of the great heroes of the *chansons de geste*. Guillaume, count of Toulouse and duke of Aquitaine, served as Charlemagne's closest lieutenant in the campaign against the Moors (or more probably the Basques) in Spain. In mourning for his wife, Guillaume renounced his wealth and titles to retire as a hermit to this deserted area. Here, he founded the monastery in 804 and received, as a gift from Charlemagne, what was said to be a piece of the True Cross. It rests on the altar of St. Guilhem and is carried in a procession through the village each year on May 3.

All that remains are the abbey church and part of the cloister. Much of the sculpture and the columns were purchased and reassembled at The Cloisters in New York. Both

---

* Henry James, *A Little Tour in France* (1882; reprint New York: Weidenfeld & Nicholson, 1987), p. 166.

St. Sernin, Toulouse (Photo: Choisnet/Maison de la France)

church and cloister are in the simple early Romanesque style.
They stand in the midst of the village beneath craggy hills at

the entrance to the wild gorges of the Verdus and the Hérault rivers.

The trail leads on to Lodève, on Route National 7. Here, part of the original cathedral still exists as the crypt of the present cathedral. The cathedral was constructed in the tenth century at the orders of the bishop and seigneur, St. Fulcran, and rebuilt in the thirteenth and first half of the fourteenth centuries. St. Fulcran, like many a monk, was also a warrior; he and his successors as bishop saw to the defenses of the town, as evidenced today by the two watchtowers of the church facade.

The great basilica of St. Sernin at Toulouse was the most important rallying point for pilgrims on the Provençal route. It was built to accommodate large crowds, with four aisles flanking the nave, a huge transept with four chapels, and five chapels radiating off the ambulatory. In the crypt are relics of scores of saints and martyrs, where, just as the pilgrims once did, you may make a "circuit of the Holy Bodies." The seven reliefs against the curved wall of the crypt are marvelous examples of early-twelfth-century monumental sculpture.

The church was built mainly of rosy brick, the local building material, though most of what you see on the interior is plastered, with joints imitating masonry. From the exterior, the powerful mass of the church, its red brick outlined in stone, rises in curves from the roofs of the chapels to the choir and transept and up to the five-story octagonal bell tower. If you visit on a Sunday, take in the enormous street fair completely surrounding the church, where you will find furniture, utensils, clothing, and handicrafts of all kinds.

St. Sernin or Saturnin, the first bishop of Toulouse, was martyred in the third century by being dragged by a bull. The nearby Church of the Taur (bull) marks the spot of his martyrdom.

From Toulouse, the trail passed through Auch, Lescar, and Oloron to join the other pilgrimage trails at Puenta la Reina in Spain and to continue westward to the goal at Compostella.

Visiting the Provençal Trail

For the Provençal trail, you might want to start out at the Jules César in Arles. Onward, consider Les Cabanettes just east of St. Gilles, the Auberge de Sanglier near Lodève, and the Noël at Réalmont. At Toulouse, there is the Grand Hôtel de l'Opéra and the d'Occitanie and the restaurants Vanel (E), Orsi, and Chez Emile. The choice of roads that parallel the trail is yours to make.

THE COMPOSTELLA TRAIL TODAY

For three hundred years, the Compostella pilgrimage and its churches and abbeys crowned the Age of Faith. The humblest pilgrim and the mightiest noble shared the vision of a unifying Christ, the adoration of neighborly saints like St. James, and the joy of creating religious art in which all participated.

But, by the fifteenth century, the pilgrimage had fallen on evil days. Commercialism had set in—if one could become a member of the Confrérie de St. Jacques just by paying dues, why bother with the long hike? Worse, the dangers of the road increased; gangsters known as *coquillards* were fleecing the pilgrims. Then, Calvin, Luther, and Erasmus attacked the whole pilgrimage structure as a monkish imposition. By the eighteenth century, special permission from one's bishop was required before the pilgrimage could be undertaken.

Compostella was revived as a shrine in the nineteenth century, and recent popes have endorsed it once again. Today, the pilgrims arrive by train, bus, or plane. But walking remains the best means of travel—not for a thousand miles, surely, but for a mile here and a mile there, a church here and a cloister there.

The Compostella trail and its churches are no longer the great unifying force in the lives of the people of southern France. But as part of history, they may affect the present. Such a thought occurred to us on an August Saturday in 1988 at the wedding of Ghislaine and Philippe at a tiny Romanesque church at Montbrun, right off the Compostella trail.

The bride was the daughter of M. and Mme. Boutonnet, who raise sheep and tobacco on the rough lands of the *causse*. Though the little commune has a total of forty telephone subscribers, more than three hundred celebrants assembled in the church for the service. For a week, the community had been sprucing up the church, decorating the porch with juniper trees and fronds of wild asparagus. All pitched in to help the family be good hosts. Gaston, the irrepressible rural mail carrier, kept interrupting the liturgy by ringing the church bells and had to be gently called to order. The curé, obviously pleased with the size and enthusiasm of his congregation, in his homily asked his flock to recall former times.

Some must have mused about the old days of pilgrimages to Compostella. After all, sitting near the bell rope, three pews over, was this same Gaston, the unauthorized bell ringer. Hadn't Gaston only last year let the whole canton in on his intention to marry Françoise by first taking her on a pilgrimage to Lourdes?

SIX

❧

Languedoc: Troubadours and Cathars

(1100 to 1300 A.D.)

O U R travels now turn from the Age of Faith to its counter-point—the era of the joyous troubadour and the austere Cathar.

The traveler in the south of France may be mystified by signs on streets and graffiti on walls in a language that is obviously not French. This is the langue d'oc, sometimes called Provençal, a mixture of archaic Latin, archaic Catalan, and perhaps a little Arabic. Until the annihilation of the Cathars in the waning days of the thirteenth century and, with it, the end of the troubadour poets and courtly society, Languedoc—the land where *oc* meant "yes"—was synonymous with the south. Even now, though French was proclaimed the official language of all France by King Francis I in 1539, langue d'oc survives as the regional patois spoken by millions in the south. If you ask someone you meet on a country lane the name of this flower or that bird, he'll likely shrug and say "I only know the patois for it, not the French.... Langue d'oc was our language before we were defeated and occupied by the French." The year 1987 marked the thousandth anniversary of the coronation of Hugh Capet as France's first hereditary king. Southern France, so far as we could determine, remained unmoved by the celebration.

LANGUEDOC'S GLORIES

From the ninth through the thirteenth centuries, Languedoc, which included much of Provence, was the political, cultural, economic, and social leader of France. It remembered the glorious days when its landscape was dappled with Roman temples, amphitheaters, villas, and forts. It remembered that the Visigoths made Toulouse their capital in the fifth century. It remembered that the counts of Toulouse, blessed by Charlemagne himself, founded the line that ruled Languedoc for four hundred years.

Languedoc's shining contributions to history include economic prosperity, political experiment, religious and social tolerance, and a culture that exalted poetry and music.

Languedoc's economic base was a large class of free farm proprietors, an inheritance from the Roman occupation. The ethnic mixture included numbers of Greeks, Jews, Saracens (Moors), and Syrians—all great traders and financiers. (In fact, the financiers of Cahors pursued their calling throughout France and the Low Countries; the word *Cahorsin* soon came to mean moneylender.) The new, upwardly mobile middle class could even assume the vestments of nobility. Thus, in Cordes, a new town set up by the counts of Toulouse in their last days, the local entrepreneur in leather or cloth could aspire to the finest house in town and the title of Grand Huntsman or Grand Falconer.

The beginnings of popular self-government appeared early

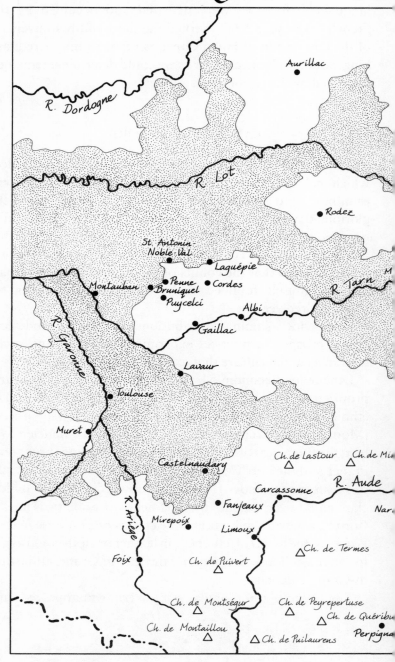

Aurillac

R. Dordogne

R. Lot

Rodez

St. Antonin-
Noble-Val

Laguépie

Montauban

Penne
Bruniquel
Puycelci

Cordes

R. Tarn

M

Albi

Gaillac

Lavaur

Toulouse

R. Garonne

Muret

Castelnaudary

Ch. de Lastour

Ch. de Mi

Carcassonne

R. Aude

Fanjeaux

Nar

Mirepoix

R. Ariège

Limoux

Ch. de Termes

Foix

Ch. de Puivert

Ch. de Montségur

Ch. de Peyrepertuse

Ch. de Quéribu

Ch. de Montaillou

Ch. de Puilaurens

Perpigna

Le Puy

R. Rhône

Avignon

Fontaine
de-Vaucluse

Tarascon

Les Baux

Montpellier

Béziers

MEDITERRANEAN   SEA

△ CATHAR CHÂTEAUX

ESTATES OF THE COUNT OF
TOULOUSE IN 1212

25 KM

in Languedoc. The counts of Toulouse maintained a loose rule over an assortment of counts, barons, and newly created municipal officials. From 1152 onward, Toulouse acquired a common council, with elected consuls or capitols, charged with civic administration with the advice of the count of Toulouse. This practice of self-government spread throughout the Languedocian towns and cities. Social and religious tolerance was the rule. Written codes modeled on Roman law governed civil transactions. Women's rights in property and inheritance were respected. The counts, good Catholics themselves, tolerated not only Jew and Mohammedan but gave shelter to heretics like the Cathars.

THE TROUBADOURS

It was in its culture of literature and learning that Languedoc most enchanted. Its magnificent courts celebrated love and chivalry in the lyric poetry of the troubadours. The word *troubadour* is generally thought to be derived from the French *trouver*, "to find," the object found being a new form of expression. But perhaps the word comes from the Arabic word *tarraba*, "to sing," or from the Greek *trope*, "to turn a phrase." Whatever the source of his name, the troubadour combined music and poetry to exalt women, romantic love, and the concept of chivalry.

Eleanor of Aquitaine caught from her grandfather William IX of Aquitaine a taste for romantic poetry, and she surrounded herself with poets at her court in Bordeaux. Her son Richard the Lion-Hearted, later Richard I of England, was a troubadour in his own right. From his prison at Dürnstein on the Danube, he wrote:

No prisoner can tell his honest thought
Unless he speaks as one who suffers wrong;

But for his comfort he may make a song.
My friends are many but their gifts are naught.
Shame will be theirs if for my ransom here I lie another
    year.
They know this well who now are rich and strong,
Young gentlemen of Anjou and Touraine,
That far from them in hostile bonds I strain.
They loved me much, but have not loved me long.

More than four hundred troubadours have left us their
poetic legacy. Arnaut Daniel, a knight of Périgord who served
at Richard's court, sang "I am Arnaut, who swims in swift
rivers against the current."

Another friend of Richard was Bertrand de Born of
Hautefort in Limousin, who succeeded in winning the heart
of a beautiful lady for whom Richard himself had conceived
a passion. Dante in his *Inferno* remembers Bertrand, carrying
his own severed head before him in penance for stirring up
discord between Richard and his father. Perhaps Bertrand was
the anonymous troubadour who wrote:

In a garden where the white thorn spread her leaves,
My lady hath her love lain close beside her,
Till the warden cries the dawn—ah, dawn that grieves!
Ah God! Ah God! that dawn should come so soon!

Arnaut de Mareuil of Limousin sang of his love for the
Countess Adalasia at the courts of Toulouse and Béziers. His
rival was Alfonso II of Aragon, who forced him to flee for his
life to Montpellier.

Bernard of Ventadour, in Corrèze, son of a servant in the
château, sang of his hopeless love for none other than Eleanor
of Aquitaine herself.

Guillem de Cabestaing indulged in the usual unrequited love
with Seremonda, Countess of Castel-Roussilon:

So fair is she for whom I sigh.
But vain are all my sighs, alas!
She heeds me not, nor deigns reply.

The count, it was said, in a fit of jealousy killed the poet, cut out his heart, and had it served at his wife's dinner. When, at the dinner's end, he told her that she had eaten her lover's heart, she replied, "My lord, you have served me so excellent a dish that I will never eat another," and threw herself from the window to her death. Neighboring nobles captured and executed the murderer. He had violated the tolerance accorded troubadours, whose convention was to praise the lord's valor and the lady's beauty—but always to stop short of her bed.

The troubadours, and indeed the entire courtly culture of Languedoc, vanished by the end of the thirteenth century. Few physical traces remain. Troubadour castles like Hautefort and Ventadour are gone, replaced by later structures. Of the original Hautefort, there remains only a Roman square column; of Ventadour, a ruined tower and donjon.

One lovely troubadour castle—Puivert (the green hill)—does still stand northwest of Quillan. Cathar knights commanded the old castle on the west of the hill, destroyed by Simon de Montfort after a three-day siege during the anti-Cathar crusade of 1210. The new castle, its donjon, towers, ramparts, and court of honor still well preserved today, was built just to the east later in the thirteenth century. Its tapestry shows a scene from the court of love, in which the ladies defined subjects suitable for troubadour songs, laid down the rules of grammar for the lovely language of oc, and pondered advice to the lovelorn in the manner of a medieval Ann Landers. In Puivert's musicians' room are eight sculptured busts of troubadours and jongleurs playing harp, lute, bagpipes, and tambourine. Puivert enjoys a splendid view over the green plain of Sault.

Tapestry of the Court of Love,
Puivert Château, Midi-Pyrénées

Another thirteenth-century troubadour castle sits on the rocky limestone butte of Les Baux-de-Provence, between Arles and St. Rémy. A road leads to the top of the butte, which is surrounded on three sides by a precipitous drop. Here, as at Puivert, the noble ladies of the court organized their court of love, holding poetry competitions for troubadours from near and far, and awarding a crown of peacock feathers to the winner. The castle was demolished at Richelieu's order in 1632, but the keep and parts of the walls remain. One April day, we were marching toward the castle when the mistral, the cold dry wind of Provence that funnels down the Rhône valley, began to blast. It tore the Michelin map from our hands and tried hard to push us off the plateau, too.

The troubadour spirit, exterminated with the Cathars in the mid-thirteenth century, was revived by two remarkable men of Provence in the fourteenth and fifteenth centuries.

The Italian poet Petrarch (1304–1368) first saw Laura, a beautiful lady but married, in a church in Avignon on April 6, 1327. He fell in love with her on the spot, but, in the platonic style of the troubadours, kept it on the endless plane of sonnets in the Italian vernacular right up to her death in 1348. He lived, meanwhile, near Avignon, at Fontaine-de-Vaucluse, site of the tremendous spring of the same name. In the village, you can visit the column erected to Petrarch and the museum on the site of his home.

Another neo-troubadour, René, is remembered as Good King René (1409–1480). Ruler of Provence for forty-six years, almost up to France's annexation of it in 1481, he was a much-loved monarch, sponsoring viticulture, promoting public health, and encouraging the arts. But René is remembered most fondly as a poet and musician. He took the troubadour code of courtly love and applied it, as the troubadours never did, to his two beloved wives, Isabelle of Lorraine and Jeanne of Laval, to whom he was married, respectively, for thirty-three and twenty-four years. You may see remembrances of Good King René in his statue at Aix, holding in his hand a bunch of grapes, in his house in the papal city of Avignon on the rue du Roi-René, and in his splendidly preserved medieval castle at Tarascon on the banks of the Rhône.

The poetic spirit of Languedoc in succeeding centuries lighted the skies of many other lands. In Italy, Dante drew his inspiration from troubadour lyrics. In Germany, the minnesingers (*Minne* means love), among them Tannhäuser and Walther von der Vogelweide, sang of romance and chivalry. Centuries later, Wagner called forth their memory in his operas. In England, Robin Hood and Maid Marian and Romeo and Juliet have clear troubadour antecedents.

The troubadours were not the only exotic fruit of medieval

The Castle of Tarascon on the Rhône
(Photo: French Government Tourist Office)

Languedoc. The world-renouncing Cathar, seemingly the antithesis of the troubadour, flourished equally in that fertile soil.

Who were these Cathars, who played such a role in the fall of Languedoc? What were their beliefs, for which they died in the fire so willingly?

THE CATHARS

Starting early in the eleventh century, the church of Rome began to encounter heretical opposition from sects that crept in from the east. The new heresies appealed to those who wanted the Bible available in their own vernacular, not just in Latin. Of these heresies, the most formidable was that of the Cathars (the Pure, often called Albigensians because Albi became one of their strongholds). Originating in Asia Minor, Greece, Bulgaria, Italy, and the Balkans, Catharism swept over Languedoc around 1150.

Catharism was a dualist creed that saw the world as divided between light and darkness; between good and evil; between the spiritual world of God and His Son, the nonincarnate Christ, and the material world of Satan and the flesh. The Cathar ministers, or *parfaits* (those seeking perfection), led austere lives of celibacy, rejecting all the outward signs of the established church—the Cross, the Mass, the saints, Mary. Their places of worship were furnished with simple tables and the Bible. Their services consisted of prayer, sermons based on the Gospel, and confession.

The Catharist creed stressed goodness, justice, and truth. The *parfaits* preached nonviolence, opposing the taking of life. Disputes were arbitrated by the *parfaits*. Lying or the taking of oaths were forbidden, and this stricture, since it included feudal oaths, challenged the foundations of feudal society.

The *parfaits* lived in poverty, as the early Franciscans had. Beyond their hooded cloaks, their cup and bowl for their meatless meals, and the Book, they had nothing. Often, they worked as weavers and artisans.

Followers of Catharism were not expected to exist in self-denial and celibacy. The *parfaits* merely asked that they try to lead good lives. Whether they succeeded or failed, the believers, or *credentes*, were entitled to the one sacrament, the consolamentum, designed to absolve them at death and place them in a state of grace awaiting a return to another life.

The women of Languedoc, tired of being considered chattels

in Catholic marriages and of being derided by the priests, played an extraordinary role in the Cathar movement. At least a third of both *parfaits* and believers were women. Great ladies such as Eleanor, countess of Toulouse, and Esclarmonde, countess of Foix, exchanged their interest in Languedocian literature for the practice of Catharism. When Esclarmonde took the Cathar side in a debate, a Catholic priest suggested that she should return to her distaff: "Lady, it does not become you to have a voice in these matters."

THE CHURCH GRAPPLES WITH HERETICS

Pope Innocent III quickly saw the danger in the new heresy. In 1205, he dispatched St. Dominic (1170–1221), a prior of the cathedral of Osma in Spain, to Languedoc to expose the Cathar errors. Dominic and his preaching friars embraced extreme poverty—in this, differing little from the Cathar priests—and walked barefoot from hamlet to hamlet debating the Cathar clergy.

In 1207, Dominic founded the nunnery of Prouille, near Fanjeaux, picking his site, it is said, because a ball of fire descended on it. The abbey, destroyed in the Revolution, was rebuilt in ponderous style in the nineteenth century. In Fanjeaux can be seen the house that was occupied, local legend has it, by Dominic from 1207 to 1215.

For all his zeal and eloquence, Dominic achieved few defections from the Cathar faithful. Toward the end of his mission in Languedoc, he realized his failure at peaceful persuasion. In his valedictory sermon to the congregation at Prouille, he confessed:

For many years I have exhorted you in vain, with gentleness, preaching, praying and weeping. But where blessing can accomplish nothing, blows may avail. We shall rouse

St. Dominic's Home, Fanjeaux

against you princes and prelates who, alas, will arm nations and kingdoms against this land.... Thus blows will avail where blessings and gentleness have been powerless.

When Toulouse fell to the crusaders in 1215, Dominic entered with them and founded the Dominican order. He died in Italy in 1221 and was canonized in 1234.

The wrath of Rome mounted as the Cathar heresy showed no signs of weakening. Mass excommunications of the Cathar clergy succeeded no more than had Dominic's gentle preachings. And the monarchs who should have been most concerned with the perceived Cathar threat, King Philip Augustus of France and Count Raymond VI of Toulouse, refused to join the anti-Cathar campaign.

For their part, many Cathars did their best to inflame the Papacy. Cathar leaders denounced the church as the corrupt and grasping Whore of Babylon. Cathar nobles at Béziers and Foix desecrated Catholic churches and seized Catholic lands.

The final straw was the slaying of the papal legate, Pierre de Castelnau, in the abbey at St. Gilles west of the Rhône. On the night of January 14, 1208, a Cathar knight, never identified, cut him down on the porch of the abbey church. The legate's body is interred in the abbey crypt.

Pope Innocent seized upon the assassination as justification for a crusade against the Cathars. To any knight who would join, he promised indulgences and such lands and loot as he could seize. He summoned Raymond VI of Toulouse to do penance at St. Gilles. There, on June 12, 1209, before the archbishops of Aix, Arles, and Auch and before nineteen bishops of Languedoc, the count was flagellated. Humbled, he swore to obey all orders from Rome and to take up the cross against his own people in the pope's new crusade.

Simon de Montfort, a baron who soon came to lead the crusade, was an adventurer from Paris whose private army was temporarily unemployed because of a lull in the wars in the Holy Land. Though Catholic and Cathar of Languedoc fought the invader side by side, they were no match for the forces pouring from northern France down the valley of the Rhône. As set forth in the *chanson de geste* of the crusader-chronicler Guillaume de Tudèle:

> It was an army marvelous and grand, twenty thousand
> knights fully armed, two hundred thousand and more

villeins and peasants, and I do not count the bourgeois and the clerics, all the men of Auvergne and from far and near, Burgundy, France, the Limousin, from the world entire they come...banners high, in serried ranks.

FIVE PHASES OF THE ANTI-CATHAR WAR

The traveler today can follow the anti-Cathar war closely because so many physical mementos remain. The five phases of the fighting can be visited in compact areas, in approximately chronological order:

- the blitzkrieg phase, along the axis of the modern Midi Canal
- the vertiginous phase, on the peaks to the north and south of Carcassonne
- the Aveyron phase, along the cliffs of that river
- the Toulouse phase, involving the fall and recapture of the Cathar metropolis
- the final holocaust at Montségur.

THE SHOCK ATTACK

The first phase, like the Nazi blitzkrieg in World War II, aimed at quick and bloody victories to discourage future resistance. Appearing before the walls of Béziers in July 1209, the converging armies of the crusaders demanded that the city council surrender to them 220 suspected heretics. When the council courageously refused, the invaders stormed the city walls and entered the cathedral square. Their leader, Abbot Arnold Amaury of Citeaux, when asked what to do with the loyal Catholics who might be found among the defenders, is said to have replied, "Kill them all; God will recognize his own."

Some 20,000 men, women, and children of Béziers, many

of whom had sought shelter in the churches, were slaughtered on July 22, 1209. The crusaders then burned the town. Of old Béziers, today only a tower of the cathedral and bits of the churches of the Madeleine, St. Jacques, and Ste. Aphrodise remain.

Five days after the holocaust of Béziers, Pope Innocent III wrote to the changeable Raymond VI at Toulouse to congratulate him on his repentance: "From a subject of scandal, you have now become an example to follow; the hand of God appears to have operated marvelously within you."

The city fathers of Narbonne, heeding the message of Béziers, shortly surrendered to the crusaders. They tried to placate their captors by turning over to them the goods of Narbonne's thriving Jewish community. Unappeased, Simon de Montfort seized for himself the duchy of Narbonne.

Carcassonne, mightiest of medieval fortresses, fell next to the crusaders. After a fifteen-day siege, its water supply ran out on August 15, 1209, and it capitulated. Its young lord, twenty-four-year-old Raymond-Roger Trencavel, was deposed and died in prison a few months later. A generation later, in 1240, Trencavel's son led an expedition to retake the citadel from its royal conquerors. Despite his stone throwers and mines, he was forced to retire.

Just south of Carcassonne, on the autoroute, is a wayside commanding a view of the fortress with its double walls, drawbridges, tall towers, and the Basilique St. Nazaire, which effectively blends Romanesque and Gothic. Thanks to the mid-nineteenth-century restoration efforts of Prosper Merimée, inspector-general of historic sites, and the architect Viollet-le-Duc, Carcassonne today looks very much as it did in 1209.

From Carcassonne, de Montfort moved on to Lavaur, perched on the left bank of the Agout near Albi. There, the

Carcassonne (Photo: Barrie Smith/Maison de la France)

Cathars resisted his siege for sixty days. After finally taking the town on May 3, 1211, de Montfort butchered eighty knights, burned "with extreme joy" four hundred Cathars who refused to accept conversion, and turned the castle's chatelaine, Dame Giraude, over to his soldiers to do with her what they liked. What they liked was to throw her down the well of the château de Plo and stone her to death.

Standing on the old foundation walls of the château overlooking the Agout, we looked at the monument that the townspeople of Lavaur had erected to the Lady Giraude. They still detest de Montfort: "*Occitan!* Defend yourself" reads the inscription on the monument. A man training his police dog nearby assured us that the lady's bones indeed still rest in the old well beneath the monument.

Close by is the beautiful pink brick cathedral of St. Alain, built by the victorious crusaders forty-two years after Lady Giraude's murder and later damaged by anti-Catholics in the

110

wars of religion and in the Revolution. Beside the cathedral is the charming Bishop's Garden, which boasts some amazing new topiary every year.

Just to the north of Lavaur, you will come upon the vineyards of Gaillac, on the Tarn (try their slightly *pétillant* white Gaillac Perlé). Gaillac fell to the crusaders without a struggle. So did Albi farther up the Tarn, where the town's bishops welcomed de Montfort.

THE BATTLE FOR THE PEAKS

Ruined Cathar forts on hilltops north and south of Carcassonne recall the second, or vertiginous, phase of de Montfort's genocidal campaign. Their stark beauty and grim history will repay you for your struggle over the back roads and occasional footpaths that you must travel to visit these eagles' nests.

To the north, Minerve, at the confluence of two deep gorges in the heart of the Minervois wine country, held out for six weeks until, on July 22, 1210, it was forced to surrender after a lucky shot from the crusader's stone thrower sealed off the town well. The little museum next to the church commemorates the burning of the 140 survivors.

Nearby, on the south flank of the Montagne Noir, you can climb a steep path to visit the ruins of the Cathar fortresses of Cabaret and Lastours. They held out until March 1211.

To the south of Carcassonne, in the foothills of the Pyrénées, are Puivert, the troubadour castle that fell to de Montfort in 1210, Termes, also taken in 1210, and Peyrepertuse, which survived until 1240.

Eastward near Pamiers is the *bastide*, or new town, of Mirepoix, with its wooden arcades. It yielded to de Montfort in 1210. He gave the lordship of Mirepoix to Guy de Lévis, one of his henchmen.

WAR ALONG THE GORGE

The third phase of de Montfort's crusade, fought out in 1211 and 1212, took place along one of southwest France's scenic marvels, the gorge of the Aveyron. A drive along the gorge will allow you to relive the story of Cathar strongholds that were conquered, betrayed, or surrendered or that somehow survived.

You might start out upstream, at Laguépie on the road from Gaillac to Cordes—then and now, a sleepy hillside town. When the crusaders arrived, the knights had prudently decamped, and the townspeople surrendered the town.

A similar fate awaited Puycelci, a walled hill town a few miles south of the Aveyron. Its ramparts and medieval houses, some in the course of restoration, make it worth a visit today. Both Laguépie and Puycelci were taken and retaken several times before the end.

Downstream is the lively town of St. Antonin-Noble-Val, where the Bonnette flows into the Aveyron from the north. Its jewel is a medieval castle built around 1125 by the viscounts of St. Antonin, feudatories of the counts of Toulouse. Later on, in 1313, it was acquired by the city consuls as a city hall, and so it has served to this day—the oldest city hall in France. Viollet-le-Duc restored it in the nineteenth century. Its tower resembles the masterwork of some Tuscan town.

As the attacking crusaders entered the town, the population attempted to flee across the Aveyron. De Montfort's men slew many in the shallows, and more drowned on the deep side. De Montfort debated whether to put the remaining inhabitants to the sword. Observing that they were employed in tilling the neighboring soil, he spared them so that he might be able to present a more productive community to his henchmen, with whom he shared the spoils.

A dozen miles downstream looms the breathtaking pinnacle of Penne d'Albigeois, its castle walls still erect at the summit. De Montfort set his blacksmiths and carpenters to work on a giant catapult to knock down the castle. It was a race against time, because many of the crusaders had grown restive and were threatening to quit the fray. To his summer patriots, de Montfort addressed a plea "not to leave the business of Christ in such great peril." Nevertheless, the *prévot* of Cologne and his German crusaders, Leopold and his Austrians, and the bishop of Laon all withdrew. On July 25, 1212, the Cathars offered to surrender provided they would be guaranteed safe-conduct. The weakened de Montfort gladly accepted and departed, leaving a small garrison in the battered castle.

Another dozen miles downstream is the well-preserved castle of Bruniquel, the oldest parts of which date back to a sixth-century Visigothic ruler. Its Cathar knights were inveigled into entrusting the castle to Baudouin, renegade brother of Raymond VI of Toulouse. Baudouin promptly turned it over to de Montfort, who rewarded him with part of the loot. Captured later by Cathar knights, the treacherous Baudouin was hanged.

TOULOUSE

The fourth phase centers on the city of Toulouse. Raymond VI had finally allied himself with the king of Aragon in an effort to save his domain. In 1213, their joint army met the crusaders at Muret, on the Garonne south of Toulouse. Pedro, king of Aragon, was slain, and the allied forces thoroughly routed. A tablet in Muret marks the spot of the battle.

In 1215, Toulouse surrendered to de Montfort, who promptly declared himself count. But the forces of Languedoc soon recaptured the city. When de Montfort again besieged it in 1218, a woman defending the walls where the law courts now stand killed him with a lucky catapult shot, "so mighty a blow it crushed his eyes and his brain, his teeth, his brow, and his jaws."

For a decade, the Cathars had a respite. But then, in 1229, Count Raymond VII of Toulouse made his peace with the French king and the church, promising to drive the heresy from his lands. After the treaty, the Inquisition was instituted, two centuries before it was taken up in Spain. The papal legate at Toulouse summoned a synod to codify the rules for exterminating heretics. Parish priests, aided by the local lords, were to conduct the searches. Because the local functionaries displayed insufficient zeal, however, Pope Gregory IX in 1233 delegated the inquisitory power directly to the Dominican Order.

The Dominicans carried out their new responsibilities with fervor. Two hundred Cathars were burned at the stake in Moissac in 1234. The inquisitors pigeonholed the Roman criminal code that had been in force for a thousand years. Trials were held in secret. The dead were tried, and their bodies exhumed from the grave to be burned. Bishop Raymond of Toulouse in 1234 had an old lady carried on her deathbed to the stake. Pope Innocent IV in 1252 officially legalized torture.

THE END

The final solution to the Cathar problem—and its fifth phase—came in 1244. Cathar knights had massacred Dominican monks of the Inquisition at the church in Avignonet near Toulouse on May 28, 1242. The Cathars had retreated to

Montségur, Midi-Pyrénées (Photo: Maison de la France)

Montségur, their stronghold in the Pyrénées, during the bloody years of the Inquisition. The troops of the French king started their siege of Montségur in May 1243.

Montségur had been constructed in 1204 as the Cathar military and ecclesiastical center. It is located on a peak of 3,937 feet; behind it rises the nearly eight-thousand-foot St. Barthélemy. The south end of the fortress was protected by a precipice. But the one hundred Cathar knights and foot soldiers, and some four hundred lay Cathars, faced a French army of ten thousand on their unprotected sides.

The crusaders' mountain troops gained a foothold near the citadel on which they could place their stone thrower. They breached the wall, and, on March 2, 1244, the garrison

115

Quéribus Château, Midi-Pyrénées (Photo: Maison de la France)

surrendered. Two weeks later, in the Field of the Burned below the fortress, 207 Cathars perished in a brushwood bonfire. Fog mercifully masked the field the day we visited the ruins of Montségur.

The last two fortified bastions of the Cathars, Puilaurens and Quéribus, east of Quillan, fell in 1255, no one knows quite how. Much of both châteaux remains on the vertiginous peaks, reachable only by stiff climbs. Puilaurens is particularly interesting; it looks like a castle, not just a ruin. As you approach by auto and, the last twenty minutes, by foot, you will marvel at the crenellated ramparts and the four towers.

116

LANGUEDOC UNDER CHURCH AND CROWN

The Inquisition continued until the fourteenth century, offering those heretics who had escaped the holocaust the choice of recanting or facing the stake. Records of the proceedings were meticulously kept by the Inquisition's court reporters. The great contemporary historian Emmanuel Le Roy Ladurie found in the Vatican library the original stenographic record of the Inquisition in the Pyrenean hamlet of Montaillou during the years 1318 to 1325. In *Montaillou,* his 1975 masterpiece about the village, he relates what the record reveals of the life and loves of the villagers.

The Inquisition was brought to Montaillou by Jacques Fournier, bishop of Pamiers and later Pope Benedict XIII. Discerning in his diocese a revival of the Cathar heresy, the bishop sent in his strike force of prosecutors and scribes. The peasants and artisans of Montaillou were interrogated not only about their Cathar leanings but about every aspect of their daily lives. Some were burned at the stake, others were imprisoned or forced to wear on their backs the golden cross of the heretic. (Incidentally, the current Montaillou telephone book contains the family names of many of the Inquisition's victims, more than six hundred years later.)

As the French crown and the Catholic church solidified their control over Languedoc, it steadily lost its courtly culture, its decentralized politics, its social tolerance, and its economic prosperity. The troubadours withered away when the petty courts that sponsored them fell to the French conqueror. Knights were soon forbidden to compose "songs of vanity." In 1280, Giret Riquier, last of the troubadours at the court of the count of Rodez, said in the twilight, "Song should express joy, but sorrow oppresses me, and I have come into the world too late."

117

Crown and church quickly put their stamp on Languedoc. In 1229, the king established the University of Toulouse .to assist the Dominicans in their heresy hunting. The victorious church sought to cow the population of Languedoc by building Gothic churches of a monumentality rivaling that achieved in Paris, Reims, and Chartres.

In Toulouse, in 1230, the Dominicans started building their Church of the Jacobins, a short walk from what is now Toulouse's central square, the Capitole. The region lacking stone, they used the red brick that is the glory of Toulouse today. The church's supporting columns in the rayonnant-Gothic style are so high and flat that they give the structure the appearance of a fortress, doubtless what the builders had in mind. The crypt contains the bones of St. Thomas Aquinas, a strange resting place, since, though a Dominican, he never set foot in Toulouse. The papacy, apparently, wanted to make sure that the new church had a reliquary capable of attracting pilgrims and their donations.

At Lavaur, in 1253, the victorious crusaders built St. Alain's near the spot where the lady Giraude had been stoned to death.

At Narbonne, in 1272, they constructed the enormous fragment of the cathedral of St. Just. Never finished, it consists of a choir 136 feet high and a transept with 194-foot towers at either end. Though lacking a nave, St. Just was a fearsome reminder to the heretically inclined of the forces arrayed against them.

At Albi, in 1252, Bishop Bertrand, who was also inspector of inquisitions for Languedoc, ordered built the great rayonn-ant-Gothic cathedral of Ste. Cécile. Of mellow red brick, its high walls supported by columns, fortified by a side tower, and embellished within by an elaborately carved stone enclo-sure called a *coro*, it towers over the countryside. Nearby, the equally ancient bishop's palace, Palais de La Berbie, houses some six hundred paintings of Henri de Toulouse-Lautrec, a native of Albi.

As a sop to the memory of the troubadours, in 1323 the crown instituted the Floral Games for poetry and prose in Toulouse. A hothouse plant, the games continue to this day in the elegant Hôtel d'Assézat.

The French king built new towns in great number throughout the southwest, not as exercises in enlightened town planning but as military outposts. Paris also absorbed the local self-government that had been established under the counts of Toulouse. Toulouse, for example, was given a parliament in 1443; its judges, however, derived their power not from city electors but from the king.

So the land of Languedoc was lost. Granted, the realities of geography might in any event ultimately have brought Languedoc into peaceful incorporation with France, without the blood and tears of the anti-Cathar crusade and the Inquisition. And how much better that would have been—for Languedoc and for France!

Visiting Troubadour and Cathar Country

The Via Dolorosa of the anti-Cathar crusade begins with the great slaughter at Béziers and the reduction of the other Cathar strong points north of the Canal du Midi and of the Autoroute des Deux Mers—Carcassonne, Lavaur, Minerve, and Lastours. The ancient cities of Carcassonne (Hôtel and Restaurant le Donjon; Logis le Trencavel; Montségur; Terminus), Narbonne (La Résidence, Maphôtel Languedoc), and Castelnaudary (Palmas) are good places to use as headquarters.

South of the canal and autoroute, the Pyrenean foothills offer equally dramatic evidence of the anti-Cathar crusade—Termes, Peyrepertuse, Mirepoix, Puivert, Puilaurens, Quéribus, and the final act at Montségur. Excellent accommodations can be found at the mountain resorts of Quillan (Pierre Luys) and Molitg-les-Bains (Château de Riell [E]), at the arcaded town of Mirepoix (Commerce), and at the wine-growing center of Limoux. At the Maison de la Blanquette in Limoux, you can buy the delicious local sparkling white wine known for many centuries as Blanquette de Limoux. With the wine, you can eat a meal prepared by the wine-growers' wives—described as "discreet and efficacious" in the inn's brochure.

For the crusade as it took place in the gorge of the Aveyron river, follow the D115, with stops at Penne d'Albigeois, St. Antonin-Noble-Val, and Bruniquel. You might try overnighting at nearby Albi (St. Antoine) or Cordes (Grand Ecuyer).

Troubadour memories can be rekindled at Puivert and at Les Baux-de-Provence, locus of no less than the Michelin three-star Oustau de Baumanière, as well as the one-star La Riboto de Taven and La Cabro d'Or. Petrarch's Fontaine-de-Vaucluse has three modestly priced restaurants "on the water." At Tarascon of Good King René's castle, you would do best at Les Doctrinaires, across the river in Beaucaire.

SEVEN

Aquitaine:
Englishmen Fight Frenchmen

(1152 to 1453)

JUST as the two great epochs of cave art and of Gallo-Roman peace came to an end with the Dark Ages, so the third creative age, roughly 1000 to 1300, of troubadour singing, live-and-let-live governing, church building, and pilgrim faring was swamped by centuries of endless wars. France saw her soil bloodied by three hundred years of dynastic wars (roughly 1152 to 1453), then by two hundred years of religious wars (roughly 1550 to 1750)—all completely senseless.

True, the three hundred years of dynastic wars saw the building of innumerable castles, fortresses, fortified churches, bridges, mills, and new towns, still there to delight the traveler. But these same wars also saw the destruction of countless noble edifices and of the fields and forests of millions of peasants whose only wish was to be left alone. Pestilence and famine rode alongside the fighting. The Black Death killed almost one-third of the south's people. And the aftermath of war left uncultivated many a farmer's fields for generations.

300 Years of War: The English in France

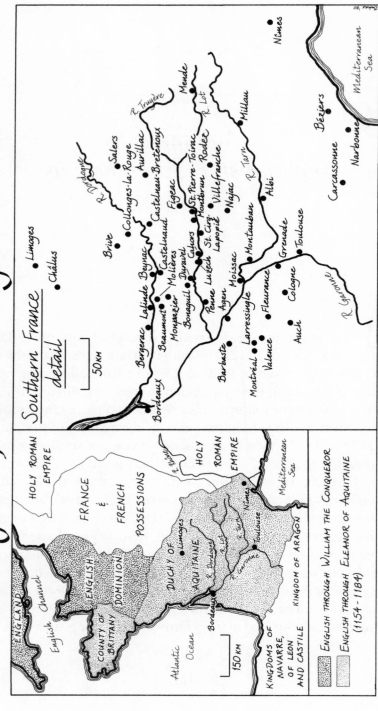

Southern France
detail

50 KM

Limoges
Châlus
Brive
Salers
Collonges-la-Rouge
Aurillac
Castelnau-Bretenoux
Figeac
Mende
R. Truyère
R. Dordogne
R. Lot
St. Pierre-Toirac
Rodez
Montbrun
Villefranche
Millau
R. Tarn
Albi
Najac
St. Cirq
Lapopie
Cahors
Luzech
Penne
Duravel
Bonaguil
Molières
Castelnaud
Montpazier
Beaumont
Lalinde
Beynac
Bergerac
Moissac
Agen
Montauban
Toulouse
Grenade
Cologne
Fleurance
Larressingle
Montréal
Valence
Barbaste
Auch
R. Garonne
Bordeaux
Nîmes
Béziers
Narbonne
Carcassonne
Mediterranean Sea

ENGLAND
English Channel
Atlantic Ocean
HOLY ROMAN EMPIRE
FRANCE & FRENCH POSSESSIONS
COUNTY OF BRITTANY
ENGLISH DOMINION
DUCHY OF AQUITAINE
Limoges
R. Rhône
R. Lot
R. Tarn
R. Dordogne
R. Garonne
Bordeaux
Toulouse
Nîmes
HOLY ROMAN EMPIRE
Mediterranean Sea
KINGDOMS OF NAVARRE, OF LEON AND CASTILE
KINGDOM OF ARAGON
150 KM

ENGLISH THROUGH WILLIAM THE CONQUEROR

ENGLISH THROUGH ELEANOR OF AQUITAINE
(1154 - 1184)

We have seen how the anti-Cathar crusade destroyed Languedoc, the southernmost part of France. With equal devastation, the dynastic wars destroyed the region just to the north of Languedoc—Périgord, Quercy, and Auvergne.

Historians refer to the period 1337 to 1453 as the Hundred Years' War. In truth, they could have called the whole period from 1150 to 1453 the Three Hundred Years' War. That France survived it—and then the religious wars, the wars of the French Revolution, the Napoleonic Wars, the Franco-Prussian War, and finally the two world wars—is a tribute to the French people and to the foundation they laid in the Golden Ages that went before.

This chapter looks at the dynastic wars during which English Frenchmen fought against French Frenchmen. The fighting started soon after the ascension of Eleanor of Aquitaine (1122–1204) to the English throne in 1152. It ended only when the English withdrew from France in 1453.

ELEANOR OF AQUITAINE

Two threads that run through the history of the south—its independence of spirit and its ability to produce striking woman figures—join in the person of Eleanor of Aquitaine.

Her life was strenuous and long. Heiress to the great duchy of Aquitaine, her grandfather and preceptor was the noble troubadour, Duke William IX; at his ducal court in Poitiers, she grew up in the company of minstrels and poets. Her father, Duke William X, had left her an orphan of fifteen when he died in the Pyrénées on a pilgrimage to St. James of Compostella in 1137. In his will, he commended her to the protection of his feudal overlord, the king of France.

The old king of France exercised his guardianship over Eleanor by marrying her to his son Prince Louis, who became

King Louis VII a few months later at his father's death. Their marriage was not a success. Louis was physically cold: according to William of Newburgh, Eleanor exclaimed "I have married a monk, not a King." For herself, she was certainly frivolous, and she may have been unfaithful. She was not displeased when Louis, disappointed at her failure to produce a male heir, obtained a divorce from her in 1152.

Within a matter of weeks, she married redheaded Count Henry of Anjou, who succeeded to the throne of England as Henry II through his mother Matilda's descent from William the Conqueror. The royal pair ruled all of Henry's Plantagenet inheritance of England and Eleanor's dowry of western France from the Channel to the Mediterranean.

The Plantagenets got their name from their habit of sticking in their hats a sprig of the *genêt*, the yellow broom-flower that you'll see on the moors of southern France. They did this to remain visible to their soldiers on the battlefield.

The marriage of Eleanor and Henry produced seven children but little happiness. Eleanor expected a say in affairs of state; Henry would not consider it. Their marriage deteriorated, until, in 1168, Eleanor left Henry and London for her native Aquitaine. At Poitiers, she set up her court of love, dedicated to Venus and the Virgin, to womanly power and to knightly respect. "Young men grow their hair long and wear shoes with pointed toes," reported a chronicle. She made magnificent progresses from castle to castle, from Poitiers to Limoges to Bordeaux.

Also at Poitiers, she had three of her four living sons. The youngest, John Lackland, stayed with Henry in England and was soon endowed with lands his father conquered in Ireland. The eldest, young Henry Courtmantel, revolted against his father. After stealing the monastery treasure from Rocamadour chapel in 1183, he fled to Martel. There, so the story goes, he gasped out his life in penance on a bed of cinders in the Maison Fabrie in the Place des Consols. Richard the Lion-Hearted, Eleanor's favorite son (described by her as "the staff of my age, the light of my eyes"), also turned against his father. Mother and son were both troubadours. Apparently a homosexual, Richard allowed no woman save his mother to come close to him. The third brother, Geoffrey Plantagenet, became count of Brittany and was killed in a tournament in 1186.

The three French sons conspired against their father with Eleanor's complicity. (Her scheming made Shakespeare consider her a Lady Macbeth: in *King John*, he calls her "a monstrous injurer of heaven and earth.") But Henry II's army put down the sons' rebellion, and, in May 1174, he dissolved Eleanor's court of love and brought her back to England a prisoner. She was kept locked up in various castles for fifteen years, until Henry's death in 1189. Accompanied by her beloved Richard, now King Richard I, she then returned to Aquitaine.

Though by then an old woman, Eleanor had not lost her vigor. On one or another family errand, she crossed the Alps into Italy and Sicily and the Pyrénées into Spain. When Richard was held for ransom in the castle-prison of Dürnstein on the Danube, she journeyed thither to secure his freedom. Toward the end, she retired to her beloved Abbey of Fontevrault, near Tours, which she made into a shelter for battered women and others who had suffered wrongs at the hand of their husbands.

She died in the abbey on April 1, 1204. Her *gisant*, or effigy, can be seen there today, book in hand, next to that of the warlike Richard, scepter on chest, and near that of Henry II. The bones of these English French disappeared during the Revolution.

Other strong mementos of Eleanor are the rock crystal and

Eleanor and Henry (?), Langon Church,
now at The Cloisters, New York

gold vase, ornamented with pearls, that she gave Louis for his
wedding present, now in the Louvre; the abbey church of St.
Denis in Paris, newly built when she and Louis attended the
dedication in 1144; a stone carving from a church in Langon
thought to celebrate Henry and Eleanor's progress through
Aquitaine in 1152, now owned by New York's Metropolitan
Museum of Art at The Cloisters; and, in Poitiers, the ancient

ducal palace where she grew up, now the *palais de justice*, and the church of Notre Dame la Grande.

"A matchless woman, beautiful and chaste, powerful and modest, meek and eloquent," the chronicler Richard of Devizes said of her. While her chastity and meekness are open to question, her other attributes clearly place her in that illustrious line of women of the south that leads from Madame Cro-Magnon through the indomitable Cathar Countess Esclarmonde of Foix to Queen Margaret of Navarre.

RICHARD THE LION-HEARTED

Eleanor's son Richard the Lion-Hearted was England's most popular king, remarkable since he spoke French, not English, and since he almost never set foot in England save for his coronation and for occasional trips to raise funds for his crusading adventures.

True to his name, Richard was a fighting man. And he could be cruel, as when he put to death 2,000 Saracen prisoners in the Holy Land. Nor did he limit his escapades to the east. Before he took off from Vézelay on the third Crusade, he managed to ravage much of southwest France. In 1188, he overwhelmed the town of Moissac because its ruler, the count of Toulouse, had imprisoned a couple of Richard's knights returning from a pilgrimage to Compostella. At Beynac on the Dordogne, he overran the ancient castle. At Penne d'Agenais near Villeneuve-sur-Lot, he built a vast tower-fortress on a five-hundred-foot peak over the Lot River. It stood until the Revolution, when it was opened as a quarry for peasants wanting to improve their homes. Its stones were further depleted for ballast for the new railroad in the 1860s, reducing it to the fragment one can see today. The young man at the

Ruins of Richard the Lion-Hearted's Tower, Penne d'Agenais

syndicat d'initiative was the only person we could find in the village who had heard of Richard. *Sic transit gloria belli.*

Richard next seized Luzech and was repulsed only at St. Cirq-la-Popie further up the Lot. Both towns reward a visit, Luzech with its donjon, St. Cirq with its ancient houses hanging on the cliff.

After his captivity in Austria, Richard reappeared in France in 1194 and set to building the gigantic fortress of Gaillard at Les Andelys on the Seine in a vain attempt to bottle up the French king, Philip Augustus, to the east. His last stand was in March 1199, at the château of Chalûs in Limousin. Word came to Richard that the lord of Chalûs had discovered a large treasure of gold on his fief. Richard demanded his cut. Refused, he besieged Chalûs and was hit on the shoulder by a new weapon, a bolt from an arquebus operated by man-at-arms Pierre Basile. Chronicler Ralph of Coggeshall told what happened:

The King lay down in his chamber and a certain surgeon in cutting the King's body wounded him seriously as he worked by the light of torches; and he could not easily find the iron head in the over-fat flesh, nor extract it without great violence. Though they applied medicines and plasters diligently, the wounds began to grow worse and turn black.

Gangrene had set in, and Richard was dead within a week. His soldiers wreaked fearful vengeance on Chalûs, hanging every defender from the battlements and flaying Pierre Basile alive. (A kindlier version has Richard on his deathbed pardoning Pierre with the words, "Enjoy the daylight as my gift.")

The granite ruins of Chalûs, used until recently for storing farm machinery, dominate the valley of the Tardoire. They are a stop on the official Route Richard Coeur de Lion, which also passes such magnificent châteaux as Rochechouart, Brie, Nexon, Jumilhac-le-Grand, Coussac-Bonneval, and d'Arnace-Pompadour, none of which had anything to do with Richard.

Richard was succeeded as king of England by his unfortunate brother John, of Magna Carta fame. By 1337, England's French dominions had been reduced to little more than Aquitaine, held as vassal of the French king.

THE BLACK PRINCE

But then there rose another English military leader, Edward the Black Prince (1330–1375), so called because of his black armor. His language, too, was French, though he did have a smattering of English. His court and military headquarters were at Bordeaux.

The Black Prince won his spurs in 1346 at the Battle of Crécy, where his father, Edward III of England, had given him command of a division. There followed years of stalemate, and the Black Prince, unable to pay his troops, in 1355 led them up the Garonne into, as Froissart records,

> what was before one of the fat countries of the world, the people good and simple, who did not know what war was; indeed, no war had been waged against them till the Prince came. The English and Gascons found the country full and gay, the rooms adorned with carpets and draperies, the caskets and chests full of fair jewels. But nothing was safe from these robbers.... [They returned to Bordeaux] their horses so laden with spoil that they could hardly move.

Pillaging as they went, they soon overwhelmed Castelnaudary. They next laid siege to Carcassonne. Observing that the fortress was protected by the river Aude and by a double wall of fortifications, Edward gave up the siege after two days but allowed his troops to loot the city outside the walls. Then on he went to Narbonne, once again savaging the houses outside the walls.

Morale thus restored, the Black Prince and his army returned to the headquarters at Bordeaux. He won a major victory over the French under King John at Poitiers on September 19, 1356. Behind spiny hedges and steep ditches, the archers toppled the French knights.

From 1363 to 1371, the Black Prince held court at Bordeaux. He built a fortress at Montauban, of which the vaulted guardroom may still be seen in the subbasement of the Ingres Museum.

His later years were weakened by illness. But, toward the end, he still had strength enough to slaughter some three thousand townspeople of Limoges because their city had rallied to his rival the French king—a slaughter presaging that by the S.S. six hundred years later at Oradour-sur-Glâne, near

Limoges, in retaliation for Maquis activity. Edward died of edema in 1376.

Many French to this day hate Richard and the Black Prince. Time and again, you will meet French who point at a crumbled ruin of a castle and snarl "Les Anglais!"

The English, for their part, are very proud of their French-speaking kings. Henry James, as English as a Bostonian can be, recalls the Black Prince's victory at Poitiers:

> The very name of the place has always caused my blood to tingle. It is carrying the feeling of race to quite inscrutable lengths when a vague American permits himself an emotion because more than five centuries ago, on French soil, one rapacious Frenchman got the better of another. Edward was a Frenchman as well as John, and French were the cries that urged each of the hosts to the fight. French is the beautiful motto graven round the image of the Black Prince, as he lies forever at rest in the choir of Canterbury: à la mort ne pensai-je mye.*

DU GUESCLIN

After Poitiers, the French fought back under their war lord, the Breton Bertrand du Guesclin (1320–1380). Short of stature, ugly as sin, du Guesclin was idolized by his followers for his courage and common sense. He beat the English by refusing the grand attack that had been so disastrous for the French at Crécy and Poitiers, instead using surprise and local superiority. By 1375, the English hold had been whittled back to Calais and the Atlantic strip from Bordeaux to Bayonne.

Du Guesclin died in 1380 of pneumonia contracted while besieging some English freebooters holed up on the rocky

---

* Henry James, *A Little Tour in France*, p. 123.

butte at Châteauneuf-de-Randon near Mende. His statue stands in the town square, and a tablet commemorates him near the stream below where he contracted his fatal illness. His entrails are buried under his effigy in the Romanesque church of St. Laurent at Le Puy, his flesh at Montferrand, his bones at St. Denis in Paris, and his heart at Dinan in his native Brittany.*

The wars grew hot again in 1415, when England's Henry V landed at the mouth of the Seine, defeated the French knights at Agincourt, and, in alliance with Burgundy, dominated northern France. Then, in 1429, came Joan of Arc to raise the siege of Orléans and have the dauphin crowned at Reims. In May 1430, she was captured by the Burgundians and sold to the English, who burned her at the stake in Rouen. Her death

---

* The southwest was not to see such warriors as Richard, Edward, and du Guesclin for another four hundred years. Then, there appeared one of Bonaparte's staunchest lieutenants, Joachim Murat (1767–1815). Born the son of a poor innkeeper at La Bastide (now Labastide-Murat) in the Lot, he soon joined the cavalry. He fought so audaciously in Italy and Egypt that he acquired not only Napoléon's confidence but the hand in marriage of Napoléon's sister Caroline. Given his marshal's baton in 1804, he won further laurels at Austerlitz, Jena, and Eylau. Finally, Napoléon made Murat king of Naples in 1808. However, Murat's fortunes fell with his emperor in 1815. His Neapolitan kingdom collapsed, and he was shot attempting almost single-handedly to recover his lost crown. Labastide-Murat preserves the inn where Murat was born and the large château on the outskirts in which his princely descendants still live. You might try to catch the horse show held every summer on the château grounds.

Southwest France produced two other famous marshals of France. Joseph-Simon Gallieni (1849–1916) was born at St. Béat near the Pyrénées. A professional soldier, he served in Morocco, Indochina, central Africa, and Madagascar. He helped establish in French colonialism a lively interest in the culture of the native peoples. Ferdinand Foch (1851–1929) grew up in Valentine near St. Gaudens. He commanded the Allied Forces in 1918 during their bloody victory over the Germans under Ludendorf. He is remembered, along with Gallieni, in a memorial statue at St. Gaudens.

inspired the French to neutralize Burgundy and force back the English. By 1453, England retained only Calais, which she lost a century later, and the Channel Isles, which she holds today.

* * *

The great sufferers in these dynastic struggles were the peasants. Murderous companies of pillagers from both sides—the French *routiers* and the English Free Companies, glorified in A. Conan Doyle's *The White Company*—ravaged the countryside. Typical is what happened at the Montbrun church, nestled next to the castle of the lord of Montbrun, back on Good Friday of 1369. As the Good Friday procession climbed the steep hill to the church, led by the priest carrying the silver crucifix, a troop of the English White Company broke in, kidnapped the lord of Montbrun, laid hands on the crucifix, and made off down the river road. The villagers pursued the brigands, cut them to pieces, and returned to the citadel with the crucifix and the lord of Montbrun intact. The lord, in gratitude, decreed that henceforth on Good Friday the peasants might escort the crucifix in the cortege and decorate the church portals with a sprig of laurel to commemorate the rescue.

Dynastic wars and their plagues and destruction left reminders throughout the south. In partial amend, the war years left mighty fortresses, romantic castles, geometric new towns, and all sorts of fortified churches, bridges, and mills.

FORTRESS-CASTLES

There are spectacular fortresses, such as Bonaguil near the Lot. This model stronghold was built by a megalomaniac feudal overlord named Bérenger de Roquefeuil toward the end of the fifteenth century. Constructed on a rocky outcrop, with massive towers, moat, drawbridge, narrow doorways, and high walls, it was built to resist any conceivable attack. None ever came, however, because by the time it was built military commanders had discovered that such a fortress could be outflanked and bypassed. More, since artillery had been perfected to the point where it could knock down the stone walls of the mightiest fortress, future forts employed low, super-thick, V-shaped earthworks. For an example of the new

Bonaguil Fortress (Photo: Bertault/Giraudon)

Fortress of Salses, near Perpignan
(Photo: French Government Tourist Office)

fortress, visit Mont-Louis in the Pyrénées near Andorra, built by Louis XIV's great engineer Sébastien de Vauban (1633–1707), the citadel at Perpignan, and the Spanish-built Salses north of Perpignan.

Another mighty fortress is Castelnau-Bretenoux, on the Cère. Its red sandstone walls and its moat date from the eleventh century. Almost destroyed by fire in 1851, it was bought in 1896 by Jean Mulieret, tenor at the Opéra-Comique. He repaired it, filled its interior with eclectic furniture and paintings, and gave it to the nation in 1932. At the music festivals held there each summer, you can have dinner on the ramparts and hear Mozart and Verdi in the courtyard.

Carcassonne in the Ariège, with its massive walls and towers, is the most renowned fortress of all. After its fall to de Montfort in 1209, it was never again taken.

Twin châteaux-fortresses glare at each other across the Dordogne, French Beynac and English Castelnaud. Each has a high donjon, where defenders could make their last stand.

Beynac has clung to its precipice over the river since Richard the Lion-Hearted's time. After remaining under one ownership for seven centuries, it was sold in 1960, needing work. Restoration goes on steadily.

Castelnaud is equally a survivor of the wars. Recently meticulously restored, it contains a fascinating museum of medieval warfare, featuring a film that links changing weaponry to the decline of medieval fortresses.

There are ruined castles perched on impossibly high cliffs, like those at Najac on the Aveyron and Penne d'Agenais on the Lot, their stones sold off to contractors during the Revolution; Cardaillac north of Figeac, a fort with two towers; and Montbrun on the Lot, one of many fortresses blown up in 1629 at Cardinal Richelieu's order in an attempt to curb the power of the country nobles.

THE BASTIDES

The wars also saw the construction of *bastides*, new towns set up by both French and English in the thirteenth century as each tried to establish a foothold in the territory of the other, the English to the north and the French to the south in a sort of geopolitical do-si-do. A *bastide*'s usual sponsors were a knight and a bishop. Inhabitants were attracted to their new homes by exemption from military service and from feudal taxes, by the right to dispose of their property to their heirs and to marry off their daughters, and by the privilege of self-government.

The *bastides* were laid out in a grid pattern, with a market, a town hall, and a church at the center and garden plots outside

Bastide of Monpazier
(Photo: French Government Tourist Office)

the walls. Typically, *bastides* also have an arcaded central square, where you can sit in the cool nursing a beer or a *citron pressé*, watching the farmers market their local produce. At Monpazier, an English *bastide*, we happened on the *Marché aux Cèpes*, where the great cocoa-brown mushrooms are sold by the case in the arcaded market. Of course, we bought the largest, which turned out to be wormy from age—a pity, because a properly selected *cèpe*, cooked rapidly in its own juices with ample garlic and herbs, exudes deliciously the musty flavor of the woods.

Other notable *bastides* set up by the English are Vianne, St. Clar, and Fourcès, with its oval marketplace and its lazy stream, south of the Garonne, and Molières, Puiguilhem, Lalinde, and Beaumont in Périgord, the latter with a fortified church.

Bastides of French settlement are Villefranche-de-Rouergue and Villeneuve in Aveyron; Montréal, Beaumont-de-

Lomagne, Cologne, Valence, Fleurance, Mirande, and Grenade in Gascony; Villefranche-du-Périgord, Villeréal, Monflanquin, and Castillonès in Périgord; and Mirepoix south of Toulouse.

MEDIEVAL TOWNS

How different from the checkerboard streets of these new towns are the winding lanes of the south's earlier medieval towns. These originated, variously, in Roman camps, abbeys, and nobles' feudal castles and their surroundings. Typical of the medieval towns worth a visit is Collonges-la-Rouge near Brive, once the administrative capital of Turenne. Master masons chiseled from the local red sandstone a massive Romanesque church, a market hall, and exquisite tiny châteaux.

Salers near Aurillac was the center for Auvergne's lawyers and "nobles of the robe." Its medieval and Renaissance structures were built of gray volcanic rock topped with slate fish-scale roofs. The deserted medieval town of Peyrusse-la-Morte in Aveyron has impressive towers, tombs, and a basilica. St. Antonin-Noble-Val on the Aveyron boasts an arcaded *hôtel de ville*, Martel a crenellated belfry and round corner towers, Figeac its treasury with gallery open to the sun (*soleilho* is the word for these galleries in langue d'oc), Uzerche its pepper-pot towers, Gourdon its old houses near St. Peter's church, Carennac on the Dordogne its Tour de Télémaque and sculptured church, the ancient duchy of Uzès in Provence its palace. With their fine inns and restaurants, these medieval towns are tourists' paradises.

Peyrousse-la-Mort, Aveyron

FORTIFIED VILLAGES, CHURCHES, BRIDGES, AND MILLS

A particularly enchanting memento of the dynastic wars is the fortified medieval village, in which the villagers could stay safe, immured within a miniature castle-fortress. The most perfect example is La Couvertoirade, just off the N9 south of Millau, described in chapter 5. Almost as fine is tiny Larresingle just west of Condom on the D15. Complete with moat,

Fortified Village of Larresingle

drawbridge, keep, chapel, and walls of wheat-brown stone, it was built by the bishops of Condom to safeguard their visitors. The inhabitants today put on a lively fête in the summer and sell their excellent Armagnac the year round.

Another offshoot of the dynastic wars is the fortified church. Good examples can be found at Rudelle north of Figeac on the N140, Beaumont in Périgord on the D660, St. Pierre Toirac along the Lot on the D662, Duravel north of Puy-l'Evêque on the Lot, Villefranche-de-Rouergue on the D922, Villeréal and Monflanquin on the D676 in Périgord, and Monpazier on the D660. Frequently, as at St. Pierre Toirac, the fortifications are a fourteenth-century graft on an eleventh-century church.

Still another offshoot is the fortified bridge, most notably, the fourteenth-century Pont Valentré over the Lot at Cahors.

Its three towers stand 140 feet above the river. The Old Bridge over the Tarn at Montauban is also fortified.

Barbaste near Henry IV's Nérac has a splendidly fortified mill. Another well-preserved fortified mill is at Cougnaquet in the Lot.

Visiting Fortified Places

Mementos of the bloody three hundred years are scattered from Chalûs (try Moulin de la Gorce at La Roche) in the Limousin, where Richard the Lion-Hearted met his end, to Châteauneuf-de-Randon in the Cévennes, scene of du Guesclin's death; from the volcanic mountains of Auvergne to the green hills of Gascony.

However, most of the archaeological evidence of the war years—the fortified castles, *bastides*, villages, churches, bridges, and gristmills—can best be observed in two compact areas: the northern, made up of Périgord and Quercy between the rivers Dordogne and Lot, and the southern, comprising Gascony west of Toulouse and generally north of the river Garonne. Most of this was once the heart of Eleanor's duchy of Aquitaine.

The travel itinerary to the northern sector includes the fortress-castles of Bonaguil and Biron in Périgord, Castelnau-Bretenoux and Castelnaudary in Quercy, and Najac (Belle Rive) on the Aveyron. The English *bastides* of Monpazier and Beaumont, the French *bastides* of Villeneuve-sur-Lot and Villeréal, the fortified church at Beaumont, and the neighboring fortified bridges at Cahors and Montauban (try the restaurant Ambroisie) should not be missed.

We made our headquarters at the Voyageurs in Beaumont—somewhat noisy as the trucks roar by in the night but well worth it for a gourmand dining room worthy of the red accolade of "good inexpensive food" bestowed by Michelin. Other choices could be the Esplanade at Domme or the Commerce at Villefranche-du-Périgord, itself a *bastide* town.

The southern sector, land of corn, plum, and early vegetables, is also full of *bastides*. Fourcès is especially winning, with its moat and its crescent main street. Other Gascon *bastides* bear the names of medieval Europe's great cities—Fleurance, Grenade, Cologne, Valence. Near Condom and Nérac is the fortified village of Larresingle and the fortified gristmill of Barbaste. A good choice for a headquarters is the France at Auch or the de Bastard at Lectoure.

Other reminders of the dynastic wars can be found as an extra dividend in the suggested itineraries for other chapters. The Gallic trip up the Lot in chapter 3, for example, will also retrace the adventures of Richard the Lion-Hearted as he rampaged from Penne d'Agenais to Luzech to St. Cirq-la-Popie. The castles near the Dordogne can be visited in connection with the painted cave explorations of chapter 2. And many of the medieval towns and *bastides* described in this chapter crop up during the tours of the Gallo-Roman days in chapter 4, of the Compostella trail in chapter 5, of the anti-Cathar crusade in chapter 6, and of the Resistance fighting in chapter 11.

EIGHT

❦

The Renaissance in the Midi: Châteaux and Mansions

(1453 to 1562)

THREE hundred years of internecine war, with its destruction, plagues, and famines, brought to a sickening end the Age of Faith that had glowed so gloriously after the year 1000. Moreover, the church, which had inherited the power and glory of Rome, now had to compete with an increasingly powerful king and with ambitious nobles. Finally, a weary people was disgusted with the church's role in the anti-Cathar crusade and the Inquisition, with its internal squabbles during the removal of the papacy to Avignon from 1309 to 1377, with the extravagance of the palace of the popes and the luxurious mansions of the cardinals in Avignon, and with its sale of indulgences and general corruption.

The devastated south was in no position to generate a new golden age to succeed those of the caves, the Gallo-Romans, and of Languedoc. Instead, it could only play host to two great movements that had their origins outside France—the Renais-

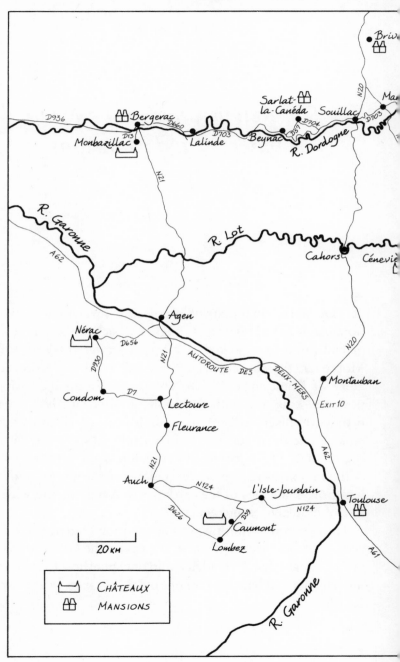

Briv

Sarlat-
la-Canéda Souillac Ma

N20

D936 Bergerac

Monbazillac D660 D703 D57 D704

Lalinde Beynac R. Dordogne D703

N21

R. Garonne

R. Lot

A62

Cahors Céneviè

Agen

Nérac D656 AUTOROUTE DES DEUX-MERS

D930 N21 N20

Condom D7

Lectoure Montauban

Fleurance Exit 10

N21 A62

Auch N124 l'Isle-Jourdain Toulouse

D626 N124

Caumont D39 A61

Lombez

20 KM

⊔ CHÂTEAUX

🏰 MANSIONS

R. Garonne

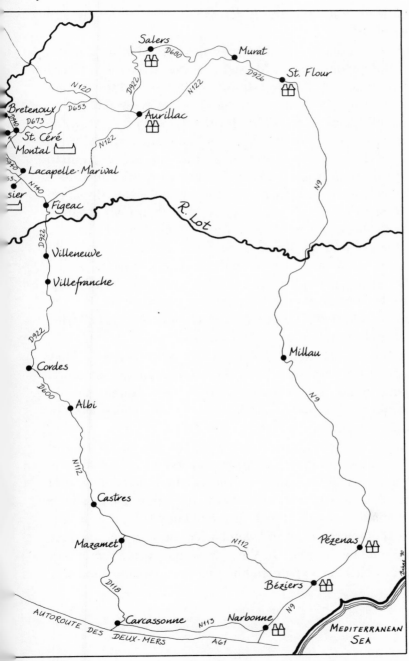

sance from Italy and the Reformation from Germany and Switzerland.

The Renaissance in southern France, though it produced a Michel de Montaigne, a Margaret of Navarre, and a Henry IV, not to mention some exquisite châteaux and town mansions, was at once too derivative and too short-lived to generate a new age of creativity. As for the Reformation, it was an unmixed disaster, bringing hideous civil wars for thirty years after 1562 and religious persecution that persisted right up to the Revolutionary guarantee of freedom of religion in 1789.

Scarcely were the French kings free of English interlopers in 1453 than they turned to foreign wars of their own. Louis X in 1473 wrested Perpignan from the kingdom of Aragon. Sovereignty went back and forth, until Perpignan finally became French with the Treaty of the Pyrénées in 1659.

Italy, now controlled by the Hapsburgs of Austria and Spain, became an even more tempting target for the French. Louis XI, Charles VII, Louis XII, and finally Francis I all tried their hands at invasion. And all were eventually driven back, with Francis declaiming: "All is lost save honor!" They brought back with them Renaissance ideas and architecture, Italian cooking, and an assortment of venereal diseases.

The ideas of the Italian Renaissance sprang from a series of events—the fall of Istanbul to the Turks in 1453, creating refugees who brought to Rome and Florence Greek art and the Greek ideas of Plato, Aristotle, and Socrates; the discovery of America in 1492 and, with it, the gold that sustained several centuries of inflationary growth; the invention of printing in 1454, making possible the diffusion of knowledge and expansion of commerce. Men and women, it appeared, were capable of unlimited greatness. Da Vinci drew man as the center of a circle; Michelangelo painted him of a size matching God's.

Assier Château (Photo: Paillasson/Giraudon)

RENAISSANCE CHÂTEAUX

The old-style fortress-castle of the Middle Ages, with its grim towers and slit windows, had become obsolete with the perfection of siege artillery in the fifteenth century. The Renaissance castle of the sixteenth century, with its high chimneys, steep roofs, decorated facades, bays with twisted pilasters open to the light, spacious windows, outside staircases, and pepper-pot turrets, was for living. Royalty and the greater nobles imported Italian architects and sculptors to build their vast châteaux at the Louvre in Paris, at Fontaine-bleau, and on the Loire. Lesser nobles of the south followed suit with smaller castles, full of light and suitable for homes for Renaissance aristocrats. The traveler to southern France will want to visit a number of Renaissance châteaux, Renaissance not only in architecture but in the lives of the men and women who built them. Seven are particularly notable.

Assier, north of Figeac, was the work of Galiot de Genouillac, munitions maker to Francis I. Returning rich from the disastrous Italian campaigns of 1535, he built his massive castle with the best Italian designers and craftsmen. Three of its four wings were destroyed in the Revolution; the remaining wing has been punctiliously restored. Nearby, the royal can-noneer built his church, adorned with sculptures depicting the deadly effect of cannon fire!

Not far off, near St. Céré, is the gem-like castle of Montal. It was built from 1523 to 1534 by the devout Jeannette Montal for her soldier son Robert, off at the Italian wars. Killed in action, he never saw the jewel box his mother had prepared. She caused the legend "No more hope" to be engraved on the entablature outside the room in which she waited for him in vain. Especially lovely are the Renaissance staircase and the facade, with its seven carved busts of the Montals.

Montal, which had suffered throughout the centuries, was bought in 1908 by the Shell Oil tycoon Maurice Fenaille. He painstakingly restored it and then gave it to the state, with the proviso that his heirs would have the right to live there from time to time. The neighborhood has been enriched by several other sensitive private restorations of the public patrimony: the medieval Castelnau-Bretenoux by the operatic tenor Jean Mulieret; Renaissance Belcastel, de la Treyne, and Les Milandes on the Dordogne, the last owned after World War

Château les Milandes, Dordogne
(Photo: French Government Tourist Office)

II by Josephine Baker of New York and the Folies Bergères; and the Tower of St. Lawrence at St. Céré, by the tapestry artist Jean Lurçat.

A third notable Renaissance château is Cénevières, on the Lot River. When Flottard de Gourdon returned after fighting in Francis I's Italian campaign, he enlarged his medieval fortress by adding a Renaissance gallery, staircase, and dormer windows. The present chatelain and his numerous grandchildren invite the public once a summer to a concert of Renaissance music in the tapestry-hung, candlelit library.

The Renaissance château at Nérac reflects the tastes of

Uzès Château (Photo: Uzès Syndicat d'Initiative)

Henry IV and his grandmother, Margaret of Navarre. We shall return to Nérac in chapter 9.

A fifth memorable Renaissance château is the ducal palace of Uzès, in Provence, with its classical facade and staircase constructed in 1550.

A sixth is Gordes, in the Vaucluse, with its mullioned windows and ornate chimneypiece. The castle houses abstract paintings by the geometric colorist Victor Vasarely.

The seventh is Caumont, on the Save River west of Toulouse, with its brick buildings and six towers almost enclosing the central court. It took its present form under the duke of Epernon, an adviser of Henry IV, whose most famous suggestion was that Henry become a Catholic and thus ensure a tranquil reign. The château, open to the public in July and August, contains a roomful of memorabilia of Henry IV. The charming chatelaine, the vicomtesse de Castelbajac, whose family has lived at Caumont for four hundred years, plays hostess to everyone from Britain's Queen Mother to a busload of American senior citizens. "We can do without a bathroom," she says, "but not without a chapel."

The south has many other Renaissance châteaux scattered about. For a profusion, try the Richard the Lion-Hearted route in Limousin, touching Rochechouart, Brie, Nexon, Jumilhac-le-Grand with its pepper-pot towers, Coussac-Bonneval, and d'Arnac-Pompadour, now a state stud farm.

RENAISSANCE MANSIONS

At the start of the sixteenth century, the blue-green lettucelike *pastel* plant (woad) flourished in the countryside to the east of Toulouse. Crushed and allowed to decompose into *coques* (shells), *pastel* yielded a lovely blue juice. Three centuries earlier, the Cathar artisans had used it to dye their textiles. The merchants of Toulouse went wholesale and marketed the dye throughout Europe. The boom turned into a bust in 1550 with the import of a superior dye, indigo, from America. But, for a while, their new prosperity enabled them to build splendid Renaissance mansions—with towers just like the nobility's, lots of windows for light, and a garden for the family—in Toulouse and throughout the fertile land of Cocagne (where the *coque* grew).

A tour of Toulouse mansions should include:

- d'Assézat, used today to house Toulouse's academies of poetry, law, and medicine. Its columns follow the Doric, Ionic, and Corinthian orders. The top floor is unfinished because the owner, a Protestant *pastel* merchant, sensed troubles ahead for those of his religion.

- de Bernuy, now a *lycée*. Its octagonal stair tower is the highest in Old Toulouse.

- de Pierre, currently apartments. It is adorned with statues of women, including one without arms, like the Venus de Milo.

- Nupces, now offices, with its brick arch of triumph.

- de Vieux Raisin, now a doctor's clinic. "I live by reason, the rest belongs to the dead" proclaims the lintel. The original owner was a city councilman and thus entitled to a few fanciful variances from the building code.

- de Brucelles, a tiny mansion owned by a gentleman from Brussels.

- du May, now the Museum of Old Toulouse.

House of the Three Wet Nurses, Narbonne

Renaissance Mansion, Sarlat (Photo: Maison de la France)

Other towns have their own Renaissance mansions.
Narbonne has the delightful House of the Three Wet

Nurses, splendidly endowed caryatids (five of them, actually) that make a magnificent Renaissance window.

Sarlat, in Périgord, was the home of Etienne de la Boétie, friend of Michel de Montaigne and, like him, a true man of the Renaissance. Montaigne wrote his essay on friendship in memory of la Boétie, who died young. Asked why they loved each other, Montaigne replied, "Because I am I, and he is he." La Boétie's is just one of Sarlat's splendid Renaissance homes. Another is the Hôtel de Maleville.

Brive, in lower Limousin, has several Renaissance mansions near the cathedral, among them the Tour des Echevins and the Hôtel de Labenche; Rodez has the Musée Fenaille; Tulle its Maison de Loyac; Pézenas in lower Languedoc, grown rich in the trade in wool cloth and as the seat of the estates-general of Languedoc, its great Renaissance mansions with sculptured niches and interior colonnaded courts available for self-guided walking tours.

Other Renaissance constructions worth seeing include the Grande-Place in Salers in Auvergne, a perfectly composed Renaissance plaza, complete with fountain and pepper-pot towers. Elsewhere in Auvergne, at Aurillac and St. Flour, are two more fine Renaissance town houses, both called Maison Consulaire and both now museums. As for churches, the south is the land of the Romanesque, with just a sprinkling of Gothic. But even here, you can find Renaissance additions to late-Gothic churches at Auch and Lectoure in Gascony.

Visiting Renaissance Châteaux and Mansions

Figeac (Hôtel des Carmes), Sousceyrac (Au Dejeuner de Sousceyrac), or St. Céré (Paris et du Coq Arlequin) are good headquarters from which to visit the Renaissance châteaux at Assier, Montal, and Cénevières. Nérac (Hôtel du Château), Gordes (Domaine de l'Enclos [E]) in the Vaucluse and Uzès

(Emeraude) are recommended headquarters for Renaissance touring farther south.

Toulouse (Grand Hôtel de l'Opéra [E], Vanal, Orsi) should be the headquarters for the nearby château of Caumont, for its own splendid Renaissance mansions, and for the farm of Ste. Julia with its *pastel* mill, and Magren with its *pastel* museum.

For accommodations at other cities with Renaissance mansions, try Midi and Le Régent at Rodez, Europe at St. Flour, Remparts at Salers, St. Pierre at Aurillac, and Toque Blanche at Tulle.

NINE

Navarre:
The Religious Wars

(1562 to 1610)

As the sixteenth century and the Renaissance advanced, the Reformation was sweeping westward from Germany and Switzerland. Reformers like Luther, Zwingli, and Calvin were inveighing against the corruption of the Catholic church. The people, they insisted, were capable of reading the Bible for themselves.

Though the Huguenots were outnumbered by Catholics in France by twenty to one, they were strong in the south. They attracted nobles, like the houses of Bourbon and Navarre, who were often more concerned with power than with theology; enterprising members of the new middle class, who appreciated the Huguenot approval of thrift, saving, and profit; intellectuals who responded to the humanism of the reformers; and peasants and artisans who believed deeply in their new faith and resented the church's sale of indulgences. An important reason for Reformist strength in the southwest was the memory of Catharism and the crusade against it three centuries earlier.

While England was achieving greatness under Elizabeth, France was being torn apart by a series of religious wars—eight of them from 1562 to 1593. From 1562 on, militant Catholics, led by the Guise family of Lorraine, tried to incite a series of weak Valois kings and their queen mother Catherine de Medicis to genocidal war against the Protestants. Sometimes the Guises would prevail, as when they slaughtered a church full of Huguenots at Vassy in Champagne in 1562, or when they massacred Huguenots throughout France on and after St. Bartholomew's Day in 1572, or when they formed the Holy League in 1576 to combat not only Protestants but the monarchy they deemed soft on Protestantism. Typically, the Protestants would secure a reprieve or an amnesty until the next outbreak of hostilities.

By the time of the next building boom, under Louis XIII, XIV, and XV, centralized government in Paris, Versailles, and the north had triumphed. In the meantime, the religious wars throughout France took a fearful toll on churches and castles, sacked and burned by Catholics and Protestants alike.

THREE FEROCIOUS CAPTAINS

Southwest France, in particular, suffered. The Catholic Captain Blaise de Monluc in his memoirs boasted of how many Protestants he had strung up on the gallows. Accused by his fellow Catholics of unnecessary brutality, Monluc recalled his services to France in the wars against the English, the Italians, and, finally, the Huguenots. Before he died in 1574, he was made a marshal of France.

Three châteaux, still lived in and not much changed since Monluc's day, evoke his memory. At St. Puy, southeast of

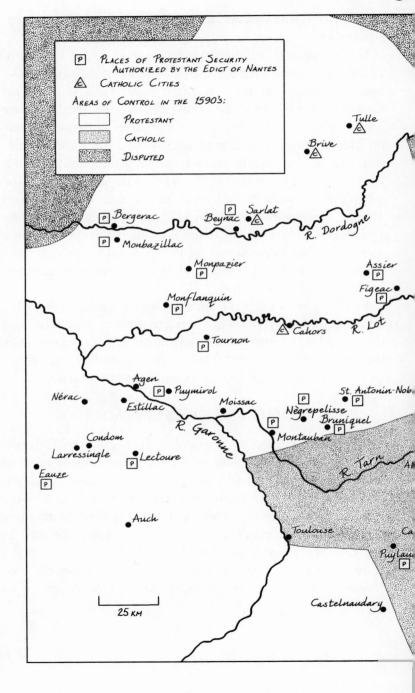

The Re

PLACES OF PROTESTANT SECURITY
AUTHORIZED BY THE EDICT OF NANTES

CATHOLIC CITIES

AREAS OF CONTROL IN THE 1590's:

PROTESTANT

CATHOLIC

DISPUTED

Tulle

Brive

Bergerac

Beynac

Sarlat

R. Dordogne

Monbazillac

Monpazier

Assier

Figeac

Monflanquin

Cahors

R. Lot

Tournon

Agen

Puymirol

St. Antonin-Nob

Nérac

Estillac

Moissac

Négrepelisse

Bruniquel

R. Garonne

Montauban

Condom

Larressingle

Lectoure

R. Tarn

Eauze

Auch

Toulouse

Ca

Puylau

25 KM

Castelnaudary

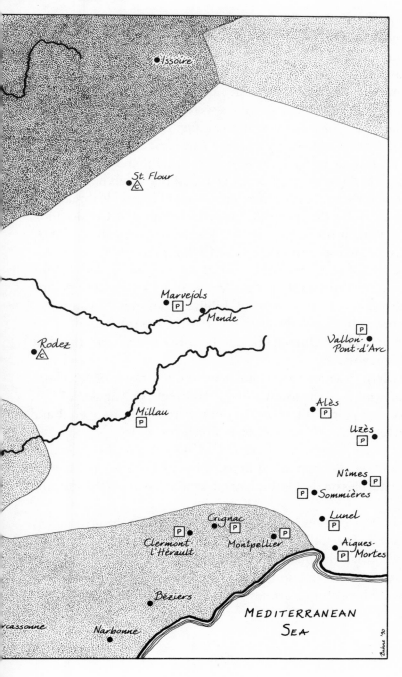

Issoire

St. Flour
Ⓒ

Marvejols
Ⓟ
Mende

Rodez
Ⓒ

Vallon-
Pont-d'Arc
Ⓟ

Alès
Ⓟ

Uzès
Ⓟ

Millau
Ⓟ

Nîmes Ⓟ

Ⓟ Sommières

Clermont-
l'Hérault
Ⓟ

Gignac
Ⓟ

Montpellier
Ⓟ

Lunel
Ⓟ

Aigues-
Mortes
Ⓟ

cassonne

Béziers

Narbonne

MEDITERRANEAN
SEA

Budros '90

Condom, and at Cassaigne, southwest of Condom, he spent time, respectively, as a young boy and as an invalid recuperating from a hideous wound received during the battle of Rabastens. The castles are inhabited today by hospitable families who will show you around and sell you their excellent Armagnac. Monluc's last days were spent at tree-shaded Estillac south of Agen, where his effigy tomb of white marble may be seen. (His body has long since disappeared.)

Protestant warriors were no less cruel than their enemies. Captain Montgomery destroyed Catholic churches and abbeys at Flaran, Lescar, Montauban, and Figeac. He threatened the same for the splendid Catholic cathedral at Condom but was bought off by the townsfolk's timely payment of 30,000 francs. He was executed by the Catholics in 1574.

Further east was the scene of operations of the equally ferocious Protestant Captain Merle. In 1576, he captured and burned Issoire in Auvergne, killing thousands of Catholics. Shortly afterward, the Catholics returned, burned Issoire once again, and slaughtered thousands more Auvergnats—this time Huguenots.

Merle was less successful with the hill town of St. Flour, thirty miles to the south. On the dark night of August 9, 1578, his men gained the ramparts but were soon discovered and driven off. St. Flour was never taken.

Further south, Merle seized Mende, today the capital of France's least populated department of Lozère. He blew up the steeples on the Gothic cathedral and destroyed the splendid bell.

In Provence, in 1562, Huguenots set fire to the great abbey church of St. Gilles, mutilated the sculpture on the west front, and hurled the monks to their deaths in the crypt. The next year, the Reformation stronghold of Orange was seized and looted by Catholic armies. To add to the destruction, a series

Arcades, Place Nationale, Montauban
(Photo: Maison de la France)

of pestilences struck down both Catholic and Protestant. In Villeneuve, in Aveyron, the Black Death returned in the sixteenth century and forced the townspeople to flee.

Beyond the ruins of churches and castles, how can today's traveler evoke memories of the religious wars? We suggest a walk through the old cities of Cahors, a Catholic stronghold, and Montauban, a center of Protestantism. Or a wine tasting at Monbazillac Château, with its Protestant Museum. Or a visit to the habitats of two who tried to conciliate the warring religions—Montaigne and his round tower and Henry of Navarre (later, king of France) and his castle at Nérac.

MONTAIGNE AND HIS TOWER

Interjecting a voice of sanity amid all the destruction was Michel de Montaigne (1533–1592). From his family château at Montaigne on the lower Dordogne, he wrote essays in his library in the round tower. Though the château burned a century ago, the library survived. You can visit it and the gardens today.

In his library, Montaigne was king: "There is my seat, there is my throne. I endeavor to make my rule therein absolute, and to sequester that only corner from the community of wife, of children, and of acquaintance." On the ceiling and rafters you can see emblazoned Montaigne's typical skepticism: "What Do I Know?" "The pro and the con are both possible." "I suspend judgment; I examine."

Though a Catholic, Montaigne was a friend of the Protestant Henry of Navarre, the tiny kingdom straddling the border of France and Spain. Henry was a guest at Montaigne's château in 1584 and slept in his bed.

Montaigne always sought a peaceful outcome to the religious wars and acted as honest broker between the French monarchy and Henry. Of heretics, he said: "After all, it is setting a high value on our opinions to roast people alive on account of them." Though he had his porter leave the castle gates unlocked, saying "I have a thousand times gone to bed imagining I should, the very same night, have been betrayed or slain in my bed," he kept his equanimity even as the religious battles raged about him.

Ironically, it was the Catholic army, 20,000 strong, that inflicted the most material harm on Montaigne. In 1585, while besieging Castillon, a neighboring Protestant town on the Dordogne, it pillaged Montaigne's lands: "I had on the one hand the enemy at my door, on the other hand the freebooters, worse enemies."

* * *

HENRY OF NAVARRE

But common sense was not enough to bring religious peace to France: it took the talents of a great politician, Henry of Navarre (1553–1610), who became Henry IV of France.

He was earthy from the start. His mother sang an ancient Gascon madrigal to him as he entered the world, then his grandfather promptly rubbed Henry's newborn mouth with garlic and washed it down with a swig of good amber Jurançon. He lived a barefoot boyhood, more suited to a Huckleberry Finn than to a future ruler of France.

In battle he was brave, his white plume showing the way. Macaulay has him say:

> Press where ye see my white plume shine, amidst the
> ranks of war
> And be your oriflamme today the helmet of Navarre.

He personally led his troops against Cahors in 1580 in reprisal for a massacre of Protestant worshipers there, fighting hand to hand and house to house for four days. He is believed to have billeted at the half-timbered Maison Henry IV in the old town.

His political tactics were flexible; he shifted his allegiance between Catholicism and Reformism several times. After ascending to the throne in 1589, he solidified his hold by converting finally to Catholicism in 1593. "Paris is worth a Mass," he supposedly said. His greatest achievement, when peace came, was to issue on April 13, 1598, the Edict of Nantes, which guaranteed freedom of religion for Protestants and provided them with security centers in Montauban, the center of the Reform movement, and in Nègrepelisse, St. Antonin-Noble-Val, Bruniquel, Marvejols, Castres,

Puylaurens, Montpellier, Millau, Uzès, Nîmes, and Aigues-Mortes.

Henry's reign brought not only peace but prosperity. Under the leadership of finance minister Sully, roads and canals were built, industry and agriculture encouraged.

Henry's weakness was the ladies. By one count, he managed to pack fifty-six mistresses into his fifty-seven years. Toward the end, in 1609, he became enamored of the beauteous sixteen-year-old Charlotte de Montmorency, wife of his natural son, the prince de Condé. He was only just dissuaded by his advisers from pursuing her to Holland. Henry was assassinated in 1610.

The small market town of Nérac in Gascony, where Henry maintained the court of Navarre, is the place to catch a whiff of his history today. Three wings of his Renaissance château on the Baïse River were destroyed in the Revolution, but the

Château of Nérac (Photo: Bertault/Giraudon)

Fortified Mill, Barbaste, Gascony
(Photo: Bertault/Giraudon)

fourth still stands. Its octagonal tower encloses a staircase leading to an open gallery with twisted pillars.

Over the Baïse River is a Venetian-style bridge, and nearby are old houses where once lodged men like Calvin and Sully. Along the right bank is the Promenade de la Garenne and what was once the royal garden, where Shakespeare probably set his *Love's Labors Lost*—"Navarre. A Park, with a palace in it."

Along the Baïse reclines the marble statue of Fleurette in her fountain. She was the sixteen-year-old who, according to legend, was seduced by the nineteen-year-old Henry and drowned herself when he abandoned her. "To that love she gave her life; Prince Henry gave it but a day" is the lament engraved on her memorial.

Four miles north of Nérac, on the Gélise, lies the four-towered fortified mill of Barbaste, where Henry often visited and where he stationed a garrison.

THREE REMARKABLE QUEENS

Nérac's castle was built, added to, and lived in by three of the sixteenth century's most fascinating women—Henry's grandmother, Margaret of Angoulême, queen of Navarre (1492–1549), his mother, Jeanne d'Albret, also queen of Navarre (1528–1572), and his wife for twenty-seven years, Margaret of Valois, "Queen Margot" (1553–1615), daughter of the king of France.

The first Margaret—the Margaret of Margarets, the Pearl of Pearls, she was called—was the older sister of King Francis I. By marrying Henry d'Albret of Navarre in 1527, she became queen of Navarre. With her patrician nose, half-closed eyes, and her Mona Lisa smile, she was a vision to look upon. She was also learned in seven languages, a poet, and a protector of scholars. Among her many writings is *The Heptameron*, a collection of mildly bawdy stories told by people of her court on their way back from Cauterets, a nearby spa. She adored her brother Francis and even journeyed to Spain to help arrange his ransom. Her court at Nérac was a delight of pastorals, maypoles, verses, plays, and gardens that Margaret called her "earthly paradise."

She was a Catholic, but her religion partook of Platonic humanism and mysticism as well. She gave shelter to men like Clément Marot, the poet of Cahors, François Rabelais, who dedicated *Gargantua* to her, and even John Calvin of Geneva. Frequently—and successfully—she had to intercede with her brother to halt the persecution of one or another of her Reformer friends. When Marot was thrown into prison for eating meat during Lent, Margaret engineered his release. Once, when the monks of Paris's Sorbonne accused Margaret herself of heresy, Francis told them to desist.

Toward the end of his life, Francis I hardened his policy and began the vigorous persecution of Protestants. Margaret, her heart broken by the failure of her dream of peaceful Catholic-Protestant reconciliation in a church purified of its cruelty and intolerance, retired to a convent and died two years later.

Margaret's daughter, Jeanne d'Albret, bore little resemblance to her gentle, lovely, witty, philosophical mother. Dour, tight-lipped, fanatical, and tough, she was said to be feminine in gender alone. Queen of Navarre at her father's death— Navarre was not subject to the Salic law forbidding the throne to women—Jeanne became an enthusiastic convert to Protestantism in 1555. She left the royal court at Paris in order to escape participation in the Mass and the company of her husband, Antoine of Bourbon, when he abjured the Huguenot faith.

From 1562 to 1572 Jeanne reigned at Nérac. Her mother's pastoral dances and games were no more. Instead, churches became temples; the little kingdom's revenues were put at the

*Wedding of Henry IV and Queen Margot, 1572; painting by
Regnier (Photo: Bibliothèque Nationale, Giraudon)*

service of the prince de Condé and his Protestant army; statues
of the saints were smashed; priests were imprisoned or
hanged.*

Jeanne, the Protestant, and her enemy Catherine de Medicis,
the Catholic, performed a remarkable feat of matrimonial
realpolitik: the match of Jeanne's Protestant son Henry and
Catherine's Catholic daughter Margaret of Valois, both nineteen. Catherine hoped that Henry's marriage to a pretty and
lively Valois princess would win him for Catholicism; Jeanne

---

* Jeanne was not the only militant Protestant noblewoman of the era.
Jeanne de Genouillac, daughter of the lord of Assier, armorer to Francis I,
converted to Protestantism. She entertained Calvin at her château and raised
a private Protestant army that controlled much of the upper Lot valley,
including Capdenac, Cardaillac, Béduer, Latronquière, and Rocamadour.

that an alliance with the royal Valois family might enable Henry to be the first Protestant king of France. Jeanne, in Paris to do her wedding shopping, died in June 1572, two months before the wedding and the St. Bartholomew's Day massacre.

Margaret of Valois, Henry IV's "Queen Margot," further immortalized in Alexander Dumas's novel, was Catholic but tolerant of Reform. Her black hair, black eyes, and splendid figure made her strikingly attractive. Witty, beautiful, elegant, lettered, she was flirtatious to the point of nymphomania. She and Henry had not been consulted about their marriage, and their mutual infidelities soon made it one in name only.

Nonetheless, she left Paris to join Henry at the court in Nérac from 1578 to 1584. There, she revived the outdoor plays and revels of the first Margaret. Though she maintained her Catholicism, she corresponded with Montaigne on ways of finding peaceful reconciliation for the warring faiths. She carried on with Henry's courtiers, recalling in her *Memoirs* that "the king my husband was surrounded by a fine troop of lords as handsome as the most gallant I had seen at court; I could have nothing against them except they were Huguenots."

For his part, Henry carried on with her ladies-in-waiting, although, on off nights, he and his warriors would go off to do battle with the neighboring Catholics. Margaret was proud of Henry's derring-do: "In the capture of Cahors, my husband showed himself not only a prince of renown but a resourceful and daring captain."

At length, Henry and Margaret's brother, the king of France, decided that her amatory escapades were an embarrassment. They sent her into exile in protective custody at the château d'Usson, near Issoire in Auvergne, where she stayed from 1587 to 1605. There, she built numerous chapels and was beloved of the clergy. She also entertained visiting intellectuals and played at gallantry with the young gentlemen of the guard at the château. Nothing of the castle's structure remains today, but houses in the little village of Usson, made of huge slabs of volcanic basalt, suggest that the peasants took advantage of building materials ready to hand after Richelieu had the castle demolished in 1633.

In 1599, Margaret consented to Henry's annulment of their marriage that he might marry Marie de Medicis. From 1605 to her death in 1615, she lived in Paris, on good terms with Henry and with the people. She built a home on the rue de Seine, grew fat, and continued her loves, letters, and devotions to the end.

Truly, three remarkable women of Nérac.

Visiting Henry IV Country

The key figure of the religious wars from 1562 to 1598 was Henry IV, and the key place his palace at Nérac. The Hôtel du Château there, or the more luxurious France in Auch, would be convenient spots from which to study Henry and his three ladies—grandmother, mother, and wife. Nearby are the reminders of the ferocious Captain Monluc, notably at the château of Cassaigne.

Other reminders of the religious wars are Montaigne's library down the Dordogne and the fiercely Catholic and Protestant cities, respectively, of Cahors (Wilson, France) and Montauban (Ambroisie [restaurant only], Ingres-Midi). Both cities also offer sparkling examples of that French institution, the good hotel opposite the railway station: the Terminus in Cahors and the Orsay in Montauban, both with enterprising young chefs presiding over pleasantly furnished restaurants.

TEN

The Cévennes:
Persecution of the Huguenots

(1610 to 1789)

F RANCE'S few years of religious peace ended with Henry IV's assassination in 1610. When the Huguenots asserted the right to maintain their own armies, Louis XIII in 1621 marched his divisions to the southwest.

Only Montauban, the Protestant center of France, resisted successfully; Louis called off his siege after three months. (The guide books claim that you can still see the mark of Louis's cannonball on the fortified tower of St. James's Church; we looked hard but couldn't find it.) Montauban's charming market square, the Place Nationale, the old houses, the Pont Vieux over the Tarn built from 1303 to 1316, the bishop's palace that now houses the paintings of native son Ingres are all of the lovely rose-red brick that also distinguishes Albi and Toulouse.

Cardinal Richelieu, made Louis's prime minister in 1624, set about centralizing authority in Paris. Intendants were sent to each province to enforce the king's law and collect the king's

The Camisards' Revolt

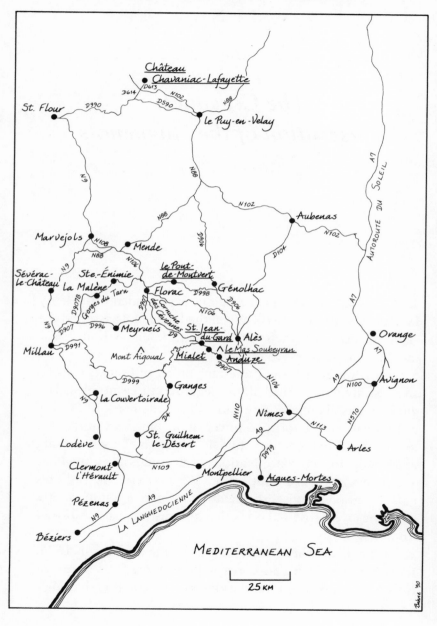

Château
Chavaniac-Lafayette

St. Flour

Le Puy-en-Velay

Aubenas

Marvejols   Mende

Sévérac-   Ste.-Énimie   le Pout-
le-Château   de-Montvert
        La Malène   Florac   Génolhac
                Gorges du Tarn
                                    Corniche des Cévennes
Millau   Meyrueis   St. Jean-
                                    du-Gard   Alès
                        Mont Aigoual   Mialet   Le Mas Soubeyran
                                              Anduze

                        Ganges   Orange

        la Couvertoirade   Avignon

Lodève   St. Guilhem-   Nîmes
                le-Désert

Clermont-   Arles
l'Hérault
                        N109   Montpellier
Pézenas   Aigues-Mortes

                    LA LANGUEDOCIENNE

Béziers

MEDITERRANEAN SEA

25 KM

taxes. All forts not on the frontier were ordered destroyed, as hundreds of ruined castles in the southwest testify. Trouble-makers were ruthlessly suppressed. When Henry of Montmorency, first noble of France and governor of Languedoc, rebelled against the crown in 1632, Louis and Richelieu went to Toulouse personally to supervise his beheading in the court of the Capitols.

The Peace of Alès in 1629 followed the fall of that Protestant stronghold to Louis XIII. It accorded the Huguenots surprisingly lenient terms. They lost the places of security granted them by the Edict of Nantes, but they kept the right to freedom of worship.

Louis XIII's two successors, preoccupied with wars and the building of palaces, were less generous. Louis XIV, observing that one and a half million Huguenots still lived in France, started after 1661 to diminish the Edict of Nantes. He successively outlawed Protestant schools, sent to the slave galleys those who aided the Huguenots, and closed Protestant churches. He instituted the infamous dragonnades, quartering in Protestant households royal troops with instructions to loot, beat, and rape.

Finally, on October 17, 1685, Louis XIV repealed the Edict of Nantes, on the grounds that it was no longer needed, France being totally Catholic! A mass emigration of 400,000 of the remaining Huguenots ensued, enriching Germany, the Netherlands, Britain, and America with talented and industrious citizens.

THE CAMISARD REVOLT

The barren hills and *causses* of the Cévennes, a center of resistance against the Nazis in World War II, also saw the resistance of the Huguenot peasants against Louis XIV's war of extermination. Camisards, so called because of their peasants' shirts, resisted to the end, sometimes armed only with pitchforks.

On July 24, 1702, a posse of fifty Camisards, attempting to free some Huguenot prisoners at le Pont-de-Montaut in the Lozère, killed the abbé de Chayla, head of the Inquisition against them. This set off a final solution by the royal troops, 30,000 against 3,000, that shortly wiped out all organized resistance.

The home of the Camisard leader Roland, betrayed and killed in August 1704, is preserved at the Mas de Soubeyran,

Musée de Roland, Mas de Soubeyran

Bridge of the Camisards, Mialet

near Alès. The Musée de Roland encompasses the simple house of Roland, his bedroom, the psalters and pulpit of the Camisards, and relics of the galleys to which many were sent. The museum is the scene of a large assembly of Protestants from all over the world on the first Sunday in September.

Nearby, and worth visiting, are Mialet, with its beautiful arched Bridge of the Camisards, where on March 28, 1703, 670 Camisards were sent to the galleys; Anduze, supply center for the Camisards, which today still boasts a splendid Protestant temple; and Castelnau castle, where Roland was killed.

A grisly reminder of the Camisard revolt is in the Tower of Constance at the medieval walled city of Aigues-Mortes. There, women Camisard prisoners were kept, one of them, Marie Durand, for thirty-seven years. She scratched on the wall of her prison: "Until Heaven, resist!"

Persecutions of Protestants continued throughout most of the eighteenth century. In 1762, Jean Calas, a respectable Protestant linen merchant of Toulouse, had a son, Marc-Antoine, who hanged himself in the family home because the profession of law was closed to him as a Protestant. (The house still stands at 50 rue des Filatiers, today a busy shopping street.) Calas was accused of having murdered his son because he was about to convert to Catholicism. Condemned by the Toulouse Parlement, he was broken, strangled, and burned at

Temple, Anduze

Tower of Constance, Aigues-Mortes
(Photo: Thierry/Maison de la France)

the stake in the public square before the cathedral. His widow fled to Switzerland and there interested Voltaire in the case. Voltaire filed appeals, wrote briefs, aroused public opinion, and, in 1765, secured an order from the Royal Council in Paris annulling the execution and reprimanding the Toulouse Parlement.

LAFAYETTE

Sanity finally descended on France. Lafayette, returning to France after the American Revolution, had promised George Washington that he would do what he could to help France's Protestants. True to his word, in May 1787, he lobbied a resolution to end proscription through the Assembly of Notables.

Lafayette, America's most respected foreign friend through his gallantry in the American Revolution and his closeness to Washington and Jefferson, remains something less than a hero in his native France. He championed the French Revolution, left it for its excesses, remained aloof from Napoléon and his wars, and in his old age helped replace the autocratic Bourbon restoration with the liberal bourgeois Louis-Philippe. An American might think that he did well by France—but his own countrymen generally regard him as flighty and insufficiently serious. Indeed, although his birthplace in Auvergne, at Chavaniac-Lafayette near Le Puy, has become a monument, it is owned and maintained by the American Lafayette Memorial Association. Visitors to the handsome château can see the room where he was born, the rose garden, and a wax museum depicting events from his life.

Lafayette's work to end bigotry did bear fruit, however. On November 27, 1787, Louis XVI signed the Edict of Toleration, a halfway step that allowed Protestants to marry, register their children, and follow a profession. With the Revolution in 1789, the National Assembly in July adopted the Declaration of the Rights of Man introduced by Lafayette, which proclaimed complete freedom of religion. And, in 1790, the National Assembly decreed that anyone descended from a Protestant expelled from France during the religious wars was entitled to French citizenship and to all its privileges. An elderly American of Huguenot descent might well consider making a test case of the law by requesting a month at a mountain spa under the French social security system.

*　　*　　*

Visiting the Cévennes

What was once the barren and deforested region of the Cévennes now flourishes as a result of the greening wrought by good forestry practices in the last century. A visit to the last stand of the Camisards can thus be combined with a unique nature experience that can recapture some of Robert Louis Stevenson's "Travels with a Donkey in the Cévennes."

For the Camisard resistance, the places to visit are the Mas de Soubeyran in the Cévennes, the temple at Anduze, and the Tower of Constance at Aigues-Mortes near Montpellier. Charming places to stay in or near the Cévennes are the Château de la Caze (E) at La Manène, the Château de Cabrières (E) at St. Jean du Gard, the Château d'Aires (E) at Meyruis, and the more moderate Hôtel de France at Mende and the Trois Barbus at Générargues near Anduze.

Resistance in the Lot

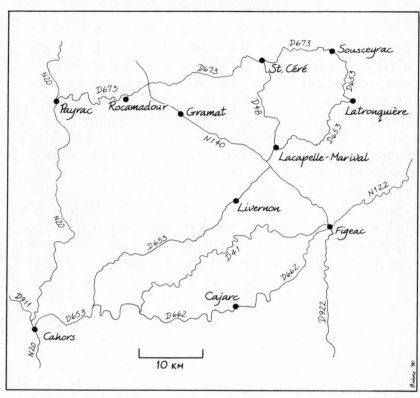

Resistance in the Massif Central

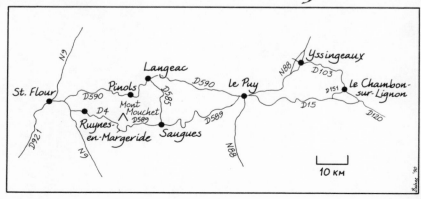

ELEVEN

───────── ❧ ─────────

The Midi Resists

(1789 to 1945)

OUR history has so far taken us through two creative ages—of the cave people and of the Gallo-Romans—through a first dark age after the collapse of the Roman Empire, through a third creative age—the Age of Faith—and then through a second dark age of wars, lasting from the Middle Ages almost to modern times. Can one identify the characteristics that allow an age to be creative rather than dark? Tentatively, three suggest themselves: a transfiguring set of ideas, freedom from war, and freedom from outside interference. The people of the cave were animated by the link between their humanity and the natural world around them. They were one people, apparently alone on the earth, with no one making war upon them or attempting to rule them. The Gallo-Romans gravitated around Roman order and Roman law. The legions provided security, and the provinces enjoyed a large measure of self-government. The third creative age was an amalgam of the universal church, Cathar otherworldly

asceticism, troubadour worldly joys, and Languedocian tolerance. This particular moment in the sun of peace and freedom
lasted until the anti-Cathar crusade and French national centralization.

From the Middle Ages until modern times, the south lan-
guished. No gripping new ideas comparable to those of her
creative ages appeared. Instead, the region was devastated by
never-ending dynastic and religious wars. Unification of the
French nation under Paris saw all the prizes go to an omnip-
otent crown, and the south of France saw what is called
modern history from the outside, looking in. It was simply not
the prime mover in the Revolution, the Napoleonic era, the
Bourbon restoration, the Empire of Napoléon III, the Franco-
Prussian War, the Third Republic, or the two world wars of
this century. Nevertheless, there can be discerned a recurring
theme in the history of the south—nothing transcendent,
surely, but still something quintessentially Midi—its refusal to
flow with the stream, born of its regional distrust of excessive
orthodoxy, militarism, nationalism, and centralization. In
small ways, that quality adds a southern flavor to many of the
great epochs of the last two centuries, from the Revolution to
the Resistance.

The Revolution was generally welcomed in the south. When
Marseille, in 1792, sent five hundred young military recruits
to defend Paris, they sang a new war song, "The Marseillaise,"
that thrilled the Paris crowds. The Revolution was also relatively mild. "In our town, we hardly knew the guillotine," the
traveler is repeatedly told. Toulouse's Capitole witnessed 44
guillotinings during the Terror; Paris's Place de la Concorde
was the scene of 16,000. Still, at the first whiff of Revolution,
peasants burned the castles of unfriendly nobles and desecrated cathedrals and abbeys, particularly church sculptures
and other graven images. In the Figeac museum can be seen a

lovely wood Christ head donated in 1978 by a family whose ancestors had bought it from a baker who had looted it from the Church of St. Sauveur in 1790.

What worked in the Revolution was land reform, whereby the 90 percent of the people who tilled the soil acquired ownership from the nobility and clergy. The Revolutionary government confiscated the lands of nobility and church, issued inflationary paper assignats against the lands' hoped-for market value, and sold the land to the peasants on easy terms. Two hundred years later, the people still have the land.

The Girondin party, made up largely of lawyers and businessmen from the Gironde district around Bordeaux, dominated the revolutionary legislative assembly during most of 1792. However, they soon fell afoul of the much more radical Jacobins, who favored a strong Paris-based government—exactly what the south had always opposed. The Jacobins triumphed; the Girondin deputies were ousted, and many went to the guillotine. Jacobin armies had to put down Girondin revolts throughout the south.

In 1989, just before the Fourteenth of July, we received a flier from the people of Figeac inviting us to celebrate with them the "Bicentenaire de la Revolution," in which all were to make "An Assault on the Bastille." This was not to be missed, and at the appointed hour we showed up at the Place de la Raison, suitably dressed in white trousers, blue shirts, and red bandannas. Following a rousing concert of the "Marseillaise" and other Revolutionary music, we formed a cortege, on horse and on foot, and with guttering torches paraded through the twisting streets of the medieval town. Arriving at the marketplace, we all joined hands and danced the carmagnole, optimistically shouting *Ça ira! Ça ira!*— roughly, "We've seen the future, and it works!" Then, it was on to the mock-up of the Bastille, on the banks of the Célé.

Gambetta Grocery Store, Cahors

With a splendid show of fireworks and a burst of cannon, the Bastille was stormed, its keepers seen to be hoisting the white flag! Over the public address system, the clear voice of Marianne was heard reading the Declaration of the Rights of Man and of the Citizen. At the stroke of midnight, a Grand Bal Populaire began in the streets.

LÉON GAMBETTA

In the days of the Franco-Prussian War, a son of the south, Léon Gambetta (1838–1882), played a leading role, helping to awaken French democracy through the founding of the Third Republic.

Gambetta grew up poor in Cahors, where his Italian immigrant father and his Gascon mother ran a mom-and-pop grocery store, the Bazar Genois. (The shop, restored, can be seen opposite the cathedral today.) A lawyer and deputy, he fought Napoléon III and his Second Empire. Radical always, Gambetta's motto was "No enemies to the Left!" Then, as the victorious Prussian army encircled Paris in 1870, Gambetta proclaimed the Third Republic. When all seemed lost, he escaped over the German lines to Tours in a hot-air balloon, then to Bordeaux, where the Parlement was sitting.

Gambetta's memorabilia may be seen in the municipal museum at Cahors and his martial statue in the Place Gambetta. Moreover, almost anywhere you go in the south, you will find a boulevard immortalizing his name. His only rival in this arena is that truly great democratic political leader, Jean Jaurès (1859–1914).

JEAN JAURÈS

That extraordinary figure, Jaurès, is a bridge between the south's historic past—freedom of thought, resistance to outside power, love for nature and for common people, opposition to violence—and her finest hour of modern times, the Resistance of World War II. In the Third Republic's Chamber of Deputies in Paris, Jaurès once recalled the brave days of the troubadours and Cathars as "the twelfth and thirteenth centuries when our intrepid and fervent southern France rose against the despotism of the Church."

Born of lower-middle-class parents at Castres, a sleepy cloth-making town on the Agout River south of Albi, Jaurès's brilliance earned him a first-class education. He became a teacher, first at the lycée in Albi, then at the University of

Garden by LeNôtre, Castres
(Photo: Service de Tourisme, Castres)

Toulouse as a professor of philosophy. At the university, he turned from a purely intellectual life to politics.

The south was dominated at the time by conservative Catholics and conservative anticlericals. Jaurès broke their hold by winning election in 1885 to the National Assembly. There, he soon distinguished himself by his moving oratory.

Back in his constituency, he became the champion of three thousand striking coal miners in nearby Carmaux, just north of Albi on the Tarn. This brought him into direct conflict with the Solages family, which owned the mines and traced its history back to 1028. The long and bitter strike was finally settled by arbitration, and thereafter, except for one short interlude, Jaurès represented the miners of Carmaux in the chamber until his death.

Jaurès was a founder of the French socialist party, which in 1981 achieved the presidency under François Mitterand. With

Emile Zola, Jaurès led the great struggle to free Captain Alfred Dreyfus, imprisoned on Devil's Island on charges of treason trumped up by an anti-Semitic army clique. In despising modern anti-Semitism, Jaurès exemplified Languedoc's historic harmony between Christian and Jew.

The great passion of Jaurès's life was the preservation of peace. Speaking to the students of his old lycée at Albi, he asked:

> Will peace always flee from us? And will the cry of mankind continue to mount toward the golden stars, always frantic but always doomed?...No!...Peace is difficult but not impossible. The appeasement of prejudices and hatreds; more comprehensive alliances and federations; international arbitration and simultaneous disarmament; the cooperation of mankind in work and learning: that will be, young friends, the greatest goal and supreme glory of the coming generation.

Jaurès soon lost his optimism. As legislator and editor, and as founder of the Socialist International, he fought to bring the Socialist parties of the other European nations into effective alliance with the French Socialists to thwart the ultranationalists and militarists and avert the looming world war. But the war came nonetheless, and on its eve Jaurès was assassinated in a Paris café by a right-wing fanatic.

The writer Romain Rolland pronounced Jaurès's epitaph:

> He has disappeared. But like the blaze of color which followed the setting of the sun, the luminous reflections of his genius, his goodness in the bitter struggle, his indestructible optimism in the face of disaster shine through the dusk gathering over a bleeding Europe.

The municipal museum in the old bishop's palace in Castres

is full of fascinating scraps from Jaurès's life. Also worth noting in Castres are the collection of paintings and prints by Goya, the garden laid out by LeNôtre, and the interesting old balconied houses along the Agout River.

THE WINE GROWERS REVOLT OF 1907

The coast of Languedoc and Provence has long produced more than half of France's wine. Times grew hard for the wine growers in 1875 when the phylloxera blight from California invaded the south, all but wiping out the vineyards. Blight-resistant rootstocks, also from California, were grafted onto the French vines and soon brought new life. Olive groves were even cut down to make way for expanded viticulture.

But devastating overproduction shortly plagued the littoral, aggravated by the competition of cheap Algerian wine. The wine growers were further outraged when the government in Paris allowed wine to be adulterated with sugar and diluted with water. Led by a populist tavernkeeper named Marcelin Albert, the peasants of Languedoc and Provence staged mass demonstrations by the hundreds of thousands in Carcassonne and Montpellier in May 1907, in protest over low prices. Albert's speech to the rally of the "Beggar's Revolt" under the walls of Carcassonne recalls the age old grievances of the Midi:

> Where once the Albigeois people defended their land and their faith under the walls of Carcassonne, the army of wine growers is today encamped—for a cause as noble as that which our ancestors in the thirteenth century died to defend. Wine growers! Cry out loud and strong: "We shall fight for our rights. The Midi wills it; the Midi shall have it!"

The Paris government in panic ordered the 17th Infantry at

Béziers into action against the demonstrators. The troops, largely sons of the embattled farmers, mutinied and were transported to Africa. The government, shaken, hastily enacted a pure food and drug law, regulating sugar and water in wine, and the crisis passed.

But overproduction has continued throughout the twentieth century. Import of cheap Common Market wine from Spain and Italy still arouses protests and the occasional dumping of wine.

THE WORLD WAR II RESISTANCE

Forty years after Jaurès's death, the south found itself uniquely suited for a role in the World War II Resistance. Perhaps the heroic struggles of Jaurès against the forces of militarism, anti-Semitism, and reaction helped inspire the south years later to struggle against the militarism, anti-Semitism, and reaction of the Germans and their collaborators.

Timing had a lot to do with the south's leading role in the Resistance. Alarmed by the Allied landings in Algeria, the Germans wanted to consolidate themselves against an invasion and did not move south until November 11, 1942. Thus the south, part of the Vichy regime of old Marshal Pétain, installed after the fall of France in June 1940, had time to put together the skeleton of a resistance force before the Wehrmacht arrived.

Also congenial to the Resistance in the south was its geography, favorable to guerrilla forces. The narrow, winding gorges and the caverns of the limestone *causses* of Quercy provided a labyrinth in which the hunted might hide. So, to the east, did the deep chestnut forests of the Ségala; the granite mountains of the Margeride in Auvergne, reforested with pine, spruce, and fir; the high desert of the Cévennes; and the fastnesses of the Alps. Everywhere, there were potential look-out points on the high hills and dispersed hamlets and abandoned farms for shelter.

Most basic of all to the Resistance in the south was the spirit of its people. Memories of centuries of cruel wars, of outside destruction of its civilization, united in the Resistance men and women of widely different views—left-leaning Catholics disenchanted with the conservative hierarchy, free thinkers, Protestants with long memories of persecution, Socialists who still thrilled to the name Jean Jaurès, unionists, young men who feared deportation to the Nazi slave labor camps, clandestine Communists, people of all classes who protested Vichy's persecution of the Jews and its banning of elections.

A significant number in the south risked torture and death for the Resistance. A few collaborated with the Germans, infiltrating the Resistance and betraying its members. But the great mass of the people of the south remained aloof and disengaged, hoping they could stay out of the troubles. We must remember that they were being fed a steady diet by Vichy, by the captive press, and by most of the Catholic hierarchy, blaming France's fall on Bolshevism, the Popular Front of Léon Blum, British perfidy, and various other scapegoats. A September 10, 1943, report from the Vichy Office of Public Information quotes "a leading citizen of Figeac" as summing up the prevailing attitude: "I would like to see the last Russian disembowel the last German, while the last Englishman expires of sheer annoyance while watching the French enjoying life!"

Later on in the occupation, the Germans' massacres and mass deportations of young men turned public opinion away from Vichy, and, as the Wehrmacht started to retreat, more and more rallied to the Resistance. But the tragic ambiguity of the majority position persists to this day. People of the south are reluctant to talk about the Resistance. Sometimes, late at night, when the fire in the hearth has burned low, you may hear an old man tell how one winter morning he found the body of his neighbor hanging from a tree down at the cross-roads.

Throughout 1943, the Resistance, known as the Maquis (for the underbrush in which they hid), grew better organized. In June 1944, the Maquis of Auvergne were able to assemble a fighting force of several thousand men on the towering Mt. Mouchet in the Margeride. This was not the isolated small-scale guerrilla warfare that the Maquis knew best but an attempt to set up a Resistance redoubt among the pines and firs of the Massif Central. Though they possessed only small arms and lacked artillery, mortars, and air cover, they fought a larger Wehrmacht force to a standstill for a week and then slipped away into the forest. The Germans retaliated by burn-ing the nearby village of Ruynes.

Farther west, in the Lot and Dordogne, the Maquis leader was Jean-Jacques Chapou, known in the underground as Captain Philippe. A thirty-five-year-old professor at the Lycée Gambetta in Cahors, he was an avid rugby player, hunter, and fisherman. His role in the Maquis partakes of the swashbuck-ling panache of those heroes of French legend, Cyrano de Bergerac and d'Artagnan.

In February 1944, feeling the need for firmer organization, better weapons, and more action, Chapou joined the Commu-nists and merged with their group, the F.T.P. (Franc-Tireur Partisans). As he wrote a friend: "I have seen the Communists at work. They have perhaps been at fault in the past, but they know how to fight and they know how to die." Chapou and his Maquis gave the German occupiers and their Vichy collab-orators a hard time. When he found the *causses* around Cahors too exposed, he took his men, in October 1943, to the forests and ravines near Sousceyrac. Denounced by collaborators, his troop was encircled by the G.M.R. (the Vichy Garde Mobile Républicaine), who called on him to surrender. Although his men were armed only with hunting guns, Chapou shouted to them—for the benefit of the G.M.R.—to open fire with their machine guns and mortar. The flummoxed G.M.R. withdrew, and Chapou was free to continue his feats of daring.

In the same month, a team of three headed by Chapou very skillfully demolished the machines in the Ratier factory in Figeac. (Ratier had been making the variable pitch propeller for the German Heinkel fighter plane.) That spring, before the Allied landing in Normandy in June 1944 and in southern France in August, the Resistance blew up vital railroad lines, including the main Paris-Toulouse line and the coal route from Decazeville. They robbed post offices of their cash. They dynamited the supplies of grain and sugar stored in dozens of town halls.

April 1944 was a particularly active month for Chapou and his Maquis. From Lacapelle-Marival, Chapou telephoned the G.M.R. barracks at nearby Figeac, claiming to be a collaborator, and asked for help against the Maquis who were allegedly terrorizing the town. The G.M.R. fell into the trap, were ambushed, and relieved of their weapons, uniforms, and boots by Chapou's Maquis. The G.M.R. detachment struggled back to Figeac in their underwear.

April 10 was the day of the monthly fair in Cajarc on the Lot, and the town was packed—then as today on fair day— with country folk buying chickens, geranium plants, kitchen utensils, shirts, dresses, shoes, and merchandise of all sorts. Suddenly Chapou and his three hundred appeared, disarmed the Vichy gendarmes, seized three collaborators suspected of betraying a Maquis detachment to the S.S., gave them a drumhead court martial, and shot them dead in front of the crowd. Chapou then telephoned the Wehrmacht headquarters in Cahors, thirty-five miles down river, and, posing as a friend, reported the Maquis attack and requested help. An armored Wehrmacht column arrived shortly, saluting as they passed Chapou's boys, many of whom were wearing stolen G.M.R. uniforms.

THE MASSACRES

Stung to madness, the Wehrmacht called for a war to the death against the Maquis. The sinister Das Reich division of the S.S., garrisoned at Toulouse and Montauban, began its march through the southwest in early May 1944. Savage reprisals commenced. On May 11 through 13, motorized columns from Das Reich assembled all men in the Figeac area aged sixteen to sixty and deported eight hundred to German slave labor camps. Nineteen people were summarily executed, and numerous houses burned. At Mende, on the upper Lot, the Wehrmacht surprised a large resistance group on the nearby Causse Méjean, killed several hundred, and marched the rest back to Bedaroux on the Lot River to be shot. A monument at the crossroads marks the spot.

The Das Reich division continued on its bloody way. On June 9, 1944, at Tulle in the Corrèze, the S.S., in reprisal for guerrilla activities the day before, seized at random one hundred men, hanged them from lampposts in front of their homes, and deported hundreds more. The next day, at Oradour-sur-Glâne, near Limoges, the S.S. machine-gunned and burned alive in the church some six hundred defenseless men, women, and children—almost the entire population. The burned-out town remains as a grisly reminder today. Other towns scorched by the retreating Germans are Lalinde and Rouffignac, near Bergerac.

Chapou Monument, Cahors

Throughout the south, plaques commemorate these horrors or pay tribute to those who died fighting the Germans or suffered torture or deportation under them. In Brive, the

Edmund Michelet museum preserves the records of the German concentration camps to which the deportees were sent.

One who died was Chapou himself, killed in a firefight while leading his troops in the Corrèze in July 1944. A sports stadium in Toulouse bears his name, and his bronze bust stands in the Place Chapou in front of the cathedral at Cahors.

One of Chapou's men is still around, forty-five years later. François Bariviera, now the leading stonemason of the canton of Cajarc, joined the Maquis early and fought in Captain Philippe's skirmishes. When not engaged in chiseling and laying out limestone, he tells tales of hiding from the Wehrmacht in caves and haystacks, meeting R.A.F. parachute drops of guns and money on the deserted *causse*, and generally keeping the enemy off balance.

Another hero of the Resistance was the tapestry artist Jean Lurçat. He left Paris in 1942 for St. Céré, where he proceeded to live a double life—as a producer of tapestries in his studio in the Tour de St. Laurent and as a clandestine leader of the Resistance. His tapestries of the day, on display at St. Céré, breathe Resistance—roosters in red, white, and blue, with the word "Liberté" woven into the designs.

The Resistance in the south, perhaps not decisive in itself, nevertheless won the praise of Churchill, Eisenhower, and De Gaulle. By blowing up railway bridges and tunnels, it prevented German troops from joining the main body of the Wehrmacht in Normandy. And, by itself, it liberated many southern cities, among them Perpignan, Aurillac, Agen, Castres, Toulouse, Montpellier, Foix, Le Puy, Limoges, and Nîmes.

But the Resistance took its purest and noblest form in the simple acts of simple people. An extraordinary example, documented in the 1989 American film *Weapons of the Spirit*, was the small town of Le Chambon-sur-Lignon, twenty-five miles east of Le Puy. There, the peasants and townspeople of this deeply Huguenot countryside saved the lives of some five thousand Jewish children and their parents by giving them refuge in their homes. They later said, "It was natural; we did nothing special"—this despite the Wehrmacht's presence and repeated visits by suspicious officials of the Vichy government. When asked about all these visitors to their beautiful hilly area, the villagers stoutly maintained, "No, we know of no Jews!" Until the Liberation, they shared with the refugees the little they had. Years later, when interviewed by the film producer, himself a refugee born in the village, they were embarrassed that risking their lives to save persecuted strangers should be thought remarkable. When we visited Le Chambon one snowy day in April 1990, we found that the villagers had not seen the movie, though they hoped it soon would be released in France.

Visiting Resistance Hideouts

The volcanic mountains and granite foothills of the Massif Central provided natural hiding places for the men and women of the Resistance. Mt. Mouchet and Mende are the places to see. At the top of Mt. Mouchet, reachable from St. Flour, there is a Resistance museum in the hunting lodge that served as the Maquis headquarters. You might stay at Michel Bras at Laguiole, the Grand Hôtel Prouhaze at Aumont-Aubrac, the Europe at St. Flour, or the Voyageurs-Vayrou at St. Chely d'Aubrac.

Westward, in the oak and chestnut forests near the Célé lie the wild ravines and gorges where Captain Philippe and his company hid out from the Nazis. Nearby, in St. Céré, is Jean Lurçat's studio in the Tour de St. Laurent, now a museum of his work. Try the Paris et du Coq Harlequin at St. Céré, the Hôtel des Carmes at Figeac, or the Au Dejeuner de Sousceyrac at the town of the same name.

Resistance Museum, Mt. Mouchet

If your travels take you west of Le Puy to Le Chambon-sur-Lignon, in search of scenes of the heroic harboring of the Jews by countryfolk, food and lodging may be found at the nearby Bois Biolotte and the Clair Matin.

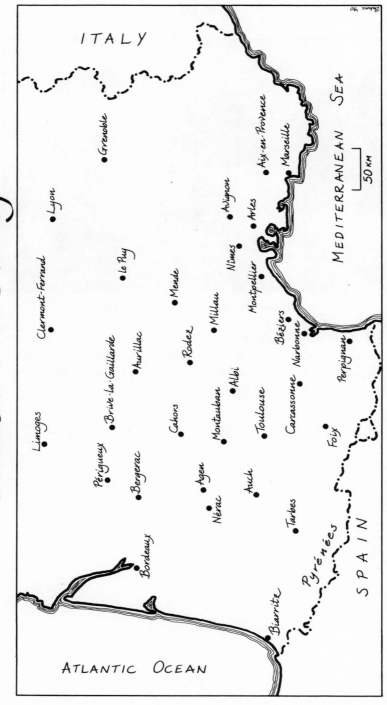

Southern France Today

TWELVE

The South Today

THE south has made great progress since World War II. Particularly in the 1980s, this had been due to a deliberate policy of decentralizing activity from Paris to backward regions. More than any other region of France, the south, with its tradition of independence, is profiting by this decentralization. Devolution may prove to be what is needed to reconcile Languedocian separatism with French nationalism. Economically, an army quartermaster depot was directed to Tulle, aerospace installations to Toulouse, national parks to the Pyrénées and the Cévennes, vast resort complexes to the Mediterranean coast of Languedoc, and improvements to the Canal du Midi. Politically, indirectly elected regional councils have been set up to foster regional development. That for the departments of the Midi-Pyrénées sits at Toulouse; that for lower Languedoc at Montpellier. As a result of the 1982 decentralization law, councils for the departments, the cantons, and the communities are being strengthened. The powers of the Paris-appointed departmental prefects, the successors of Louis XIV's intendants, have been trimmed.

You can see this post-war transformation in every Midi village. Too many people used to share too few economic opportunities. Today, many thousands have left the farm or the hamlet for jobs in Paris or the other big cities. But they do not forget their roots in "*France profonde*" and return to their patrimony for their summer vacations or to help at the harvest. Ruined farmhouses, barns, towers, and other empty buildings are being remodeled for retirees or visitors from northern France and the rest of Europe. Because the stone masons of the south have retained their traditional skills and because the

Languedocian grafitti, Limoux

Canal du Midi

departmental offices of historic preservation are commendably hard-nosed, most of the restoration is done sensitively.

Where once the housewife had to trudge down to the river to do her laundry and trudge back up again with her supply of water, today, an electric washer and running municipal water make her life easier. Where primitive communications used to leave many a farm and village totally isolated, today, the television obliterates space and time.

The two great cities of the Midi, Toulouse and Montpellier, have stirred from somnolence in the years since World War II. Toulouse shines in aerospace—the Concorde and the Ariane rocket—in fertilizer, and in electronics; Montpellier in computers, pharmaceuticals, and agribusiness. Both are vibrant

Capitole, Toulouse (Photo: Maison de la France)

cultural centers. Both have ancient and illustrious universi-
ties—Toulouse, of whose law school Montaigne is said to be
an alumnus, and Montpellier, where Rabelais went to medical
school. The University of Toulouse today has some seventy
thousand students, second only to Paris.

The Midi is rich in recently developed hydroelectric power
and natural gas. But its main sustenance remains agriculture.
There are sheep on the dry limestone *causses*, cows in the
upland meadows, ducks and geese in the farmyards. Thrifty
peasants still produce nonpareil fruits and vegetables, wheat
and corn, nuts and truffles and flowers. In addition to the huge
production of ordinary wine in the Mediterranean coastal
plain, the Midi's vineyards yield excellent reds from Cahors,
Corbières, Marcillac, Minervois, Madiran, and Buzet; whites
from Gaillac, Limoux, Bergerac; dessert wines from
Montbazillac, Jurançon, and Rivesaltes.

A charming glimpse of farm life in the premechanized Midi

is available at the Cuzals open-air farm museum at Sauliac on the Célé. There, children and grown-ups can see a donkey-powered water pump, an ox-drawn cart, a steam tractor, a duck pond, and artisans at work making everything from pots to clogs, from bread to barrels.

Given its age-old love of nature, it is not surprising that the south is in the forefront of France's growing environmental movement. In the 1970s, environmentalists blocked the expansion of an army base on the *causse* of Larzac on the grounds that it could endanger the fragile ecosystem; they are currently fighting a large hydroelectric dam on the upper Loire and the proposed corridor of the new autoroute between Brive and Montauban.

One aspect of the new France that specially delights the visitor is the decentralization of culture. André Malraux, De Gaulle's minister of culture, promulgated the concept of the museum without walls, and his successors have seen to it that adequate subsidies for music and art go to the provinces. As a result, on summer nights, you can hear a flute and harpsichord in the candlelit great hall of the castle of Cénevières on the Lot, or the splendid Toulouse symphony in the Gothic church on top of the hill in Gourdon, or the Pablo Casals festival at Prades, or an opera at Castelnau-Bretenoux on the Cère, or organ music at St. Bertrand-de-Comminges, or one of the great festivals of Provence. Almost every town, at a museum or at the *syndicat d'initiative*, has an art show in progress.

At a more popular cultural level, the rural south teems with neighborliness. Every village has its hunting club, looking after the condition of game and coverts. Expenses are defrayed by a *meschoui*, an outdoor lamb barbecue that attracts the countryfolk for miles around. Making the rounds of the *meschoui* alone will assure you of a dozen summer outings. Then there are the village fêtes and the specialties—*pétanque* for the bowlers; bicycle and motorcycle racing, hang gliding, or trap shooting for the venturesome; dancing in the streets for all ages.

More than ever today, the traveler to the Midi, as Jefferson wrote to Governor Rutledge, will return from his tour "charged, like a bee, with the honey gathered on it."

Afterword

WHEN TO VISIT

Winter in southern France is generally cold and rainy, and spring doesn't begin on a reliable basis until May, but then all becomes delightful. July and particularly August are the peak tourist seasons, but congestion is nothing like what you would find in Nice, Cannes, and St. Tropez or in the tourist havens of the north. The summer months are hot by day, for which the remedy is to stay out of the sun from noon to late afternoon, as the natives do. And autumn, well into November, is superb.

TOURS

Most visitors to southern France will travel on their own, but for those who like organization and can afford it, some guided tours are now available. In 1988, the Smithsonian Institution of Washington offered a two-week tour of the châteaux, caves, and villages of the Dordogne; Plantagenet Tours of Bournemouth, England, offered "The Eleanor Tour to Medieval France," "The Troubadour Tour to Medieval Aquitaine," and "The Plantagenet Tour to Medieval England and France"; Alumni Flights Abroad of New York offered a ten-day tour of the Dordogne.

GETTING THERE

For getting from Paris to Provence, there is now the famous TGV (Train à Grande Vitesse) running from the Gare de Lyon to Lyon, Marseille, Toulon, and Fréjus at electrifying speeds of around two hundred miles per hour. For getting from Paris to the southwest, frequent trains from the Gare d'Austerlitz to Brive, Gourdon, Cahors, Caussade, Montauban, and Toulouse are inexpensive, comfortable, and relatively fast (five to seven hours). A TGV for Paris-Toulouse is projected for the mid-nineties, cutting the travel time to two-and-a-half hours. For now, the twice-daily Le Capitole is worth the extra fare.

Lower fares are offered for four- to sixteen-day passes, for families, and for senior citizens. If you travel by night, sleepers are available (you may want something more comfortable than the second-class *couchettes* in which six strangers are racked up in triple tiers). And you may take your car along by the Autotrain.

Frequent, and expensive, air flights are offered from Paris to Marseille, Nîmes, Nice, Toulon, Toulouse, Albi, and Rodez.

GETTING AROUND IN THE SOUTH

Trains are inexpensive and comfortable in the south; the hitch is that they frequently don't go where you want to go.

Tour buses take much of the joy out of life, and regular buses may have inconvenient schedules. This leaves the bicycle, which puts you at one with the French *sportif;* walking; the Canal du Midi; or the automobile.

If you drive, here are a few hints. Familiarize yourself with the French traffic signs: they are common-sensible and meant to be obeyed. *Ralentir* or *se reculer* mean "slow down," *sens unique* means "one way," *virages* means "curves," *épingles à cheveux* means "hairpin curves," and—the best we've come across—*nids de poule,* which does not mean "chickens nesting," as we thought until we hit the holes. When engulfed on a country road by a herd of sheep tended by a bicycling farmer, yield and relax for a quarter of an hour. On the southern superhighways, try not to shudder as cars whiz past you at one hundred and twenty miles per hour. If you pass, road etiquette requires using your directional blinker before you pull out and before you pull back in.

If you are energetic, try hiking. France has more than 18,000 miles of Grande Randonnée hiking trails, each marked with red and white blazes and with its own Topo Guide, obtainable at bookstores. The trails traverse villages where simple lodging for the night is available at inns or hostels (*gîtes d'étape*). Particularly recommended are Grande Randonnées 40, 400, and 441, in the volcanic mountains of Auvergne (contact Comité Regional de Tourisme, 45 av. Julien, 63011 Clermont-Ferrand); 67–67A and 71, the Robert Louis Stevenson donkey trail in the Cévennes (contact Comité Regional de Tourisme, 12 rue Foch, 34000 Montpellier); 60, the cattle drovers' route in Languedoc (contact Comité Regional de Tourisme, 12 rue Salambo, 31222 Toulouse); and 36 in the Lot, offering a seven-mile hike from the market town of Beauregard to the restored priory of Laramière and a five-mile hike from Puy-l'Evêque to the fortified church of Duravel.

THE CANAL DU MIDI

This marvelous waterway, completed in 1689 under the direction of Languedoc's tax collector, Baron Pierre-Paul Riquet, can be both an end in itself or a means of visiting some of the Midi's great sights.

In its heyday, the canal carried the grain of the Midi farmers to market; then the train and the truck took over. Recently, however, pleasure boats have revived traffic on the canal. Barge trips by the day or week may be arranged through the Office de Tourisme, Pl. Republique, 11499 Castelnaudary, or the Syndicat d'Initiative, Donjon du Capitole, rue Lafayette, 31555 Toulouse. *The Canal du Midi*, by Odile de Roquette-Buisson (New York: Thames & Hudson, 1983), is indispensable for anyone contemplating such a trip. The canal is currently being enlarged east of Toulouse to accommodate larger boats.

Thomas Jefferson agreed that the canal is a charming way to see the Midi. "There is nothing in France," he wrote to his young friend John Rutledge, Jr., on March 25, 1789, "so well worth your seeing as the canal and country of Languedoc and the wine country of Bordeaux."

The widowed Jefferson had arrived in Paris as minister of the Continental Congress, accompanied by his eleven-year-old daughter Martha, in August 1784. He loved to travel, and his favorite trip was to southern France and northern Italy in 1787. In May, on his way back to Paris, he embarked on a barge on the canal at Sete and thus reached Carcassonne, Castelnaudary, Toulouse, Agen, and Bordeaux. His letter to his friend William Short describes the trip:

> I dismounted my carriage from its wheels, placed it on the deck of a light bark, and was thus towed on the canal

instead of the post road. That I might be perfectly master of all the delays necessary, I hired a bark to myself by the day, and have made from twenty to thirty-five miles a day, according to circumstances, always sleeping ashore. Of all the methods of traveling I have ever tried this is the pleasantest. I walk the greater part of the way along the banks of the canal, level and lined with a double row of trees which furnish shade. When fatigued I take seat in my carriage, where, as much at ease as if in my study, I read, write, or observe. My carriage being of glass all around, admits a full view of the varying scenes thro' which I am shifted, olives, figs, mulberries, vines, corn and pasture, villages and farms. I have had some days of superb weather, enjoying...cloudless skies and limpid waters: I have had another luxury...a double row of nightingales along the bank of the canal, in full song.... What a bird the nightingale would be in the climate of America! We must colonize him thither.

We got the flavor of the canal by starting early one July morning from the big basin at Castelnaudary. Castelnaudary itself has its sights—windmills and ancient churches—and its tastes, notably the cassoulet, made of patiently simmered haricot beans and preserved goose. Anatole France described a cassoulet that had been cooking for twenty years as having attained "that special amber that colors the flesh tones of the old Venetian masters." Castelnaudary's is rivaled only by those of Toulouse and Carcassonne.

Leaving Castelnaudary, our barge moved westward lock after lock over the watershed between the Mediterranean and the Atlantic. At Narouze, an obelisk marks the spot where water for the ascending and descending locks is brought by a channel from the crest of the Montagne Noir.

The land we passed through, the Lauragais, is the breadbasket of southern France. Great fields of sunflowers turned their heads to follow the sun (thus *tournesols*). The sky was violet with intense heat, but we were shielded by sycamores and cottonwoods arching over our heads. Branches hung low, and the bargeman kept crying out, "Watch your ears! Watch your glasses!"

Aboard our barge were crowds of teenagers who livened our passage by periodically taking the microphone, with many a giggle, to sing bits of popular music. One of them, an obviously retarded young girl, suddenly asked for the mike and sang with great clarity and beauty that old children's favorite, "Au Clair de la Lune." She ended with an enormous grin, hugging herself in triumph. It was only after the trip was over that we discovered that these lively, well-behaved young people were from special schools run by the French social security system for mentally or physically handicapped or orphaned children.

Locks were frequent, single or in groups of two or three depending on the height we had to reach. In this stretch, they were "manned" by a lavishly proportioned blonde in dark glasses, singlet, and split skirt. As she wound the winches, she created a great sensation.

Sailing yachts from the Atlantic came by, masts lowered, en route to the Mediterranean. At one moment, the diversity of French transport hit us: as we slipped silently through the canal's green waters, the Bordeaux-Marseille express passed a freight train on one side of the valley; just beyond lay the Autoroute des Deux Mers with its speed maniacs.

Castelnaudary is just one suitable port of entry for the Canal du Midi. To the east lie many others—Carcassonne, Narbonne, Béziers, and Sete.

Narbonne, a wine town, lies some five miles off the main canal, on the connecting Canal de la Robine. The quai where the canal barges land is right off La Cité, with its relics of the days when Narbo Martius was the first Roman capital of Gaul.

Béziers, scene of the 1210 Cathar horror, is the home town of canal-building Pierre-Paul Riquet. Béziers today is a considerable wine center, also renowned for its championship rugby football teams.

Sete, where the Canal du Midi empties into the Mediterranean, is a thriving and colorful fishing port. Lining the quais are inexpensive seafood restaurants serving excellent fresh sardines and tuna.

FOOD AND LODGING

Inns bearing the sign Logis de France or Auberges de France tend to be reliable. *Chambres d'hôte* are clean and comfortable rooms in private homes, distinguished by their green and yellow signs. Their extremely reasonable prices are due in part to their exemption from the value-added tax. *Gîtes* are similar but rentable only for longer periods, such as a week or a month. Auberges de Jeunesse are youth hostels. Finally, campsites are numerous and excellent for those with tents or campers.

Selecting a simple eating place on your own is perfectly feasible. If the local people frequent it at noon, particularly if a farmer has parked his tractor in front, you'll probably like it. Be sure to sample such local specialties as foie gras, *magret* (sliced duck breast), *confit d'oie* (preserved goose), wild mushrooms and truffles, walnut oil, cassoulet (white beans with goose and sausage), bouillabaisse (fish stew), and sheep and goat cheeses.

This book mentions a number of inns and restaurants that

we have tried and liked or heard reliably recommended. Since prices change, we have simply noted "E" when a restaurant is expensive.

The digestive system is challenged by two big meals a day. Thus, the motorist is advised to eat dinner when stopping for the night and to be content with a picnic lunch en route. Half the fun of the picnic lies in shopping at the charcuterie for a pâté or sausage, at the fromagerie for a bit of cheese, at the boulangerie for a loaf of bread, and at the épicerie for a bottle of wine or fruit juice. If one avoids the crowded coast, the south abounds in idyllic spots for a picnic.

SPAS

The south of France teems with thermal resorts that will appeal to some visitors, particularly the older ones. The baths are especially renowned for treatment of arthritic, nervous, and respiratory ailments. Scores of spas are concentrated in the hot springs regions of Auvergne (Vichy, Néris-les-Bains, Bourbon-l'Archambault, St. Nectaire) and the Pyrénées (Luchon, Cauterets, Amélie-les-Bains, Bagnères-de-Bigorre).

Some 650,000 French, aided by generous subsidies from the social security fund, take the cure each year. So soothing is the combination of the baths, the peaceful surroundings, and the fresh air, according to the social security authorities, that patients find their use of doctors and medicines reduced by one-half and one-quarter, respectively, in the year following treatment.

Just why hot water full of gases and algae should be beneficial has been a mystery since Roman times, but it does make a lot of people feel better. While you will probably not wish to take a four-week cure, you may find a four-day stopover at a spa an excellent marshaling place for your travels through history.

GUIDEBOOKS

For guidebooks, we swear by the green Michelins for Périgord-Quercy, Auvergne, Causses, Pyrénées-Roussillon, and Provence. For all of France, the Blue Guide and the guides from Penguin, Baedeker, Hachette, Birnbaum, and Fodor are all helpful. For food and lodging, the Red Michelin or Gault-Millau are great.

For maps, the detailed Michelins (75 for Bordeaux-Tulle, 76 for Aurillac-St. Etienne, 79 for Bordeaux-Montauban, 80 for Rodez-Nîmes, 81 for Avignon, 82 for Pau-Toulouse, 83 for Carcassonne-Montpellier, 84 for Marseille, and 86 for Luchon-Perpignan) are recommended, because many of the roads that you will need in order to reach out-of-the-way spots are secondary or lower, though always paved.

There are a number of worthy guides to southern France, all by British authors. The late Freda White wrote three of them a quarter of a century ago: *Ways of Aquitaine* (London: Faber & Faber, 1968), *Three Rivers of France* (New York: Arcade Publishing, 1989), and *West of the Rhône* (London: Faber & Faber, 1964). Also helpful are Richard Barber, *The Companion Guide to Southwest France* (London: Collins, 1977); Henry Mayhill, *North of the Pyrénées* (London: Faber & Faber, 1973); Andrew Sanger, *Languedoc and Roussillon* (Lincolnwood, Ill.: Passport Books, 1989), Arthur Eperon, *The Dordogne and the Lot* (Lincolnwood, Ill.: Passport Books, 1989), Roger MacDonald, *Provence-Côte d'Azur*, (Lincolnwood, Ill.: Passport Books, 1989); and James Bentley, *A Guide to the Dordogne* (London: Penguin, 1986).

Be sure to make full use of that delightful institution, the *syndicat d'initiative*, in just about every town with a population of a thousand or more. With modest government subsidies, the *syndicats* give sightseeing information, sponsor exhibitions, maintain hiking trails, house minimuseums, and distribute travel literature.

Index of Place Names

The Best Things in New York Are Free: Over 1000 Attractions and Activities That Won't Cost You a Penny
Revised Edition
By Marian Hamilton
$10.95 paper, ISBN 1-55832-031-8
400 pages

Now revised, this is the most comprehensive guide to everything that's free in New York City. This book isn't just a listing, it's an activity-oriented book catering to the most diverse interests. From film buffs to tour addicts, from children to senior citizens, there is something for everyone to enjoy in the Big Apple.

The Carefree Getaway Guide for New Yorkers: Day and Weekend Trips Without a Car
Revised Edition
By Theodore Scull
$9.95 paper, ISBN 0-916782-95-6
256 pages, maps

For restless New Yorkers, Scull describes forty day and weekend trips in New York and its environs, including Connecticut, Pennsylvania, Rhode Island, and New Jersey. The book is ideal for all sorts of travelers: students, adventurous older folks, young professionals without cars and anyone with a car who is tired of fighting New York's traffic.

Exploring Our National Parks and Monuments
Revised Eighth Edition
By Devereux Butcher
$14.95 paper, ISBN 0-87645-122-9
400 pages, black and white photographs

"This is very possibly the best available collection of photographs of our national parks. Schools and libraries will find it an admirable guide and sourcebook as will the traveler." — *Library Journal*

Going Places: The Guide to Travel Guides
By Greg Hayes and Joan Wright
$17.95 paper, ISBN 1-55832-003-2
800 pages

This book critically reviews 3000 travel guides and travel guide series ranging in subjects from gourmet tours to family vacations to safari adventures. The easy-to-use format is organized by country/region and includes three appendices which list travel bookstores, travel book publishers and travel magazines and newsletters.

A Guide to Public Art in Greater Boston
By Marty Carlock
$8.95 paper, ISBN 0-916782-94-8
192 pages, black and white photographs

The first guidebook to works of art in Boston's public spaces includes over 300 murals, statues and abstract works with information about the artist, medium and history of each piece. One hundred photographs pinpoint particular works for both the tourist and the serious student of art.

How to Take Great Trips with Your Kids
By Sanford and Joan Portnoy
$8.95 paper, ISBN 0-916782-51-4
190 pages

Traveling with kids can be fun and easy, once you know some special techniques. Whether you're driving to Aunt Helen's or flying to Zanzibar, this book offers the ABCs of planning, packing and en-route problem solving.

The Insider's Guide to Santa Fe
Revised Edition
By Bill Jamison and Cheryl Alters Jamison
$8.95 paper, ISBN 1-55832-022-9
17 pages, maps, black and white photographs

The only travel guide solely devoted to Santa Fe and its surroundings, this book delves into local history, takes you on walks along historic streets and up mountain trails and invites you to Indian pueblos and old Spanish villages. In addition, this guide describes fiestas, festivals and exhibits; art galleries and shops (rated for the excellence and depth of selection); restaurants, hotels, motels and nightlife.

Paradores of Spain: Unique Lodgings in State-Owned Castles, Convents, Mansions and Hotels
By Sam and Jane Ballard
$8.95 paper, ISBN 0-916782-76-X
256 pages, maps, black and white photographs

A companion guide to *Pousadas of Portugal,* this is the only published guide to the luxurious lodgings owned and operated by the Spanish government. The Ballards, who have visited every parador, provide detailed maps, photographs and suggested itineraries as well as lively descriptions of the accommodations and their historic settings.

The Portable Pet: How to Travel Anywhere with Your Dog or Cat
By Barbara Nicholas
$5.95 paper, ISBN 0-916782-49-2
96 pages

If vacation wouldn't be the same without your faithful friend, or you're planning to move your pet along with the rest of your household, you're headed into a maze of requirements and regulations. Find the answers to all your questions in this lively and pragmatic guide.

Pousadas of Portugal: Unique Lodgings in State-Owned Castles, Palaces, Mansions and Hotels
By Sam and Jane Ballard
$8.95 paper, ISBN 0-916782-77-8
192 pages, maps, black and white photographs

A companion volume to *Paradores of Spain,* this is the only published guide to the luxurious lodgings owned and operated by the Portuguese government. The Ballards, who have visited every pousada, provide detailed maps, photographs and suggested itineraries as well as lively descriptions of the accommodations and their historic settings.

Romantik Hotels and Restaurants: Charming Historic Hotels in Europe and America
Edited by the Romantik Hotel and Restaurant Association
$6.95 paper, ISBN 1-55832-012-2
296 pages, maps, color photographs

This book provides weary travelers with over 150 options for a dependable respite in foreign lands. Hotels and restaurants affiliated with the Romantik Association must conform to high standards. They all must be located in a historic building, under the personal management of the owner, have first-class cuisine, friendly service and a pleasant and comfortable atmosphere.

A Traveler's Guide to the Smoky Mountains Region
By Jeff Bradley
$10.95 paper, ISBN 0-916782-64-4
288 pages, maps

The first comprehensive and critical guide to southern Appalachia, a land of outstanding natural beauty and old-time graciousness. "A thoroughgoing, level-headed guide through some fascinating hills!" — *Roy Blount, Jr.*

Travel Writer's Markets: Where to Sell Your Travel Articles and Place Your Press Releases
Revised Edition
By Elaine O'Gara
$16.95 cloth, ISBN 1-55832-009-3
$8.95 paper, ISBN 1-55832-008-3
224 pages

Travel writing is a competitive business, which is why Elaine O'Gara has written this book. Novice travel writers who deserve that lucky break will discover a wealth of practical information regarding professional submission of manuscripts and photos, researching a magazine's market potential and contacting travel book publishers.

Where to Eat in Canada
Revised Twentieth Edition
By Anne Hardy
$11.95 paper, ISBN 1-55832-024-5
384 pages

This is *the* authoritative guide on the best places to eat in not just the major cities but also towns and villages all across the country. Anne Hardy, well-known restaurant critic, has been in charge of the guide for its entire twenty years of publication.